THE DEATH OF KING ARTHUR

The Death of King Arthur

translated by
SIMON ARMITAGE

faber and faber

First published in 2012
by Faber and Faber Ltd
Bloomsbury House
74–77 Great Russell Street
London WCIB 3DA

Typeset by CB editions, London
Printed in England by T. J. International, Padstow, Cornwall

A CIP record for this book
is available from the British Library

ISBN 978–0–571–24947–3

10 9 8 7 6 5 4 3 2 1

Contents

~

Introduction

~

In 410 AD the Romans withdrew from Britain, leaving the country open to attack from Germanic tribes all along Europe's north-western fringes. The pull-out was a gradual process rather than a moonlight flit, but for history to make sense it requires eras and periods separated by memorable dates and clear dividing lines rather than vague segues or blurred transitions. Viewed in those terms, it was as if the Romans had left overnight. A period of huge social turmoil was to follow, but with very little in the way of evidence or record, and it is in the shadowy, silent days of the next hundred or so years that the first glimmers and rumours of a character called Arthur are to be found.

Through the deep roots of Welsh folklore Arthur initially makes his name as a Celtic hero, defending the embattled people of the west of Britain against a variety of enemies, including the English. One of the earliest mentions of him comes in the poem *Y Gododdin*, possibly pre-dating the ninth century, in which another warlord is singled out for praise, despite being 'no Arthur', suggesting that Arthur's fame and qualities were already widely known and needed little in the way of explanation. Arthur appears in other Welsh stories, some not written down till the turn of the first millennium but with their origins dating back to a much earlier age. In the ninth-century *Historia Brittonum*, sometimes attributed to a Welsh monk, Nennius, we get the earliest 'historical' account of Arthur in action. The text describes a series of twelve battles, culminating in the Battle of Badon Hill, in which Arthur is said to have killed 960 men in one day by his own hand. Similarly, in the *Annales Cambriae*, composed not later than the tenth century, the author presents as a true historical occurrence the Battle of Camlann, during which the fatal fight between Arthur and Mordred takes place. In 1136, Geoffrey of Monmouth created the first 'biography' of King Arthur in a section of his *History of the Kings of Britain*, written in Latin. At a time when literature and history were not necessarily approached as independent disciplines, Geoffrey positions Arthur in a succession of British monarchs dating right back to Brutus. It was a popular and cleverly conceived text, pleasing to the ruling Norman elite, and one that offered a unifying and rousing version of Arthur which appealed both to Norman aspirations and to the Welsh tradition.

A poet from Jersey, Wace, introduced the concept of the Round Table in his *Roman de Brut* (1155), and not long afterwards Arthur was to receive something of a total make-over at the hands of Chrétien de Troyes, the brilliant French author of several Arthurian Romances. In keeping with the literary fashions and social tastes of the day, ideals of courtly love and chivalric code became the all-important themes, with Arthur sidelined, emasculated even, by the deeds of the amorous Lancelot in pursuit of Guinevere and the adventurous Perceval in pursuit of the Holy Grail. In these stories, honour, faith and virtue became both motive and subject, and it is interesting to consider the extent to which the popular image of King Arthur, one of Britain's greatest national heroes, is in a good part the creation of French-speaking poets.

Sometime around the end of the twelfth century, a Worcestershire parish priest by the name of Layamon wrote the long, sprawling poem *Brut*, an important moment not only in the transmission of Arthurian narrative but for English literature in general, since it was the first time that the story of Arthur had been written in the English language. Layamon drew heavily on Wace, just as Wace had drawn on Geoffrey of Monmouth, just as Geoffrey had drawn on the Welsh myths, but plagiarism, or 'intertextuality' as we might allow these days, was not only considered necessary and acceptable but often looked on as a badge of learning. Nowhere is this form of compositing more evident or successful than in the work of Sir Thomas Malory, the author of the prose work *Le Morte Darthur*, as published by Caxton in 1485. Possibly written during Malory's incarceration, the book is a classic of world literature and the text by which most people have come to know the stories of King Arthur and the Knights of the Round Table. Malory's achievement was to pull together many disparate and sometimes confusing strands of Arthurian legend and present them as one definitive and continuous storyline, and to do so in a style which had all the excitement of fiction but also the gravitas of fact. The sword in the stone, the lady of the lake, Guinevere's adultery with Lancelot: all these scenes and plots have their origins elsewhere, but it is through Malory's retelling that they have become so ingrained in our consciousness and have remained so popular.

Malory had certainly read the *Alliterative Morte Arthure* (*AMA*), the academic and unglamorous title given to the poem of nearly four and half thousand lines written sometime around 1400, of which this book is a translation. Its title distinguishes it from another poem of the same era written in lyrical eight-line verses, known as the *Stanzaic Le Morte Arthur*, and both poems could be considered part of a renewed flourishing in Arthurian literature, which included *Sir Gawain and the Green Knight*. Like *Gawain*, the *AMA* was written by an anonymous author and only one copy remains in existence, kept in the gatehouse library of Lincoln Cathedral. Because of dialect words and certain turns of phrase the author is thought to have come from the north-east midlands or possibly the north of England, though the manuscript is actually a copy, in the hand of the Yorkshire-man Robert Thornton, who may well have contributed some of his own literary and linguistic mannerisms to the poem's style and tenor. Both *Gawain* and the *AMA* are written in alliterat-ing lines which harped back to the Anglo-Saxon style of poetic composition, but unlike *Gawain*, whose plotline hinges around one moment of jaw-dropping magic, the *AMA* concerns itself with the far more down-to-earth world of warfare and poli-tics, specifically the ever-topical matter of Britain's relationship with continental Europe, and the no less relevant subject of its military interests overseas. During the Christmas celebra-tions at Carlisle, the festivities of the Round Table are rudely interrupted by a messenger from the Roman Emperor, Lucius Iberius, demanding taxes and homage from Arthur in respect of disputed territories in France and elsewhere. Rising to the challenge, Arthur and his army embark on an armed campaign which takes them almost to the gates of Rome, before Arthur is forced to turn back to deal with matters closer to home.

The *Alliterative Morte Arthure* is hardly a story of suspense, since its outcome is announced in its very title, but the manner of the King's death and the way in which every incident right from the opening passages are bound up in its conclusion are examples of sophisticated literary structure and storytelling at its very best. The tale also incorporates several subplots describing the fates of dozens of fighters on both sides of the battle lines, including Gawain himself, no longer the callow, naive wanderer outwitted by a green wizard and a wrinkled witch, but a fearsome warrior and Arthur's most trusted knight. Nevertheless, three episodes are remarkable for their vivid flights of fancy. The first describes in the most graphic detail a battle to the death between King Arthur and a hideous, cannibalistic giant occupying Mont St Michel on the French coast, who counts the beards of famous kings amongst his grisly trophies. The other two are prophetic nightmares at the beginning and then at the end of Arthur's European campaign. In the first, a monstrous bear from the east does battle with a massive dragon from the west, and in the second, the King is wooed then turned upon by an all-powerful lady as she spins Fortune's Wheel. These dream sequences are internalised, private glimpses into the conflicted mind of Arthur, in stark contrast with the rhetorical world of court and the cut and thrust of war. Through them, we begin to see Arthur as a human being rather than just a figurehead, and as a consequence his fate becomes a matter of huge drama and poignancy.

In and amongst, fight follows fight, charge follows charge, and the poem itself is a battlefield littered with horribly disfigured corpses and no end of internal organs. Once the bowing and the trading of witty insults had been dispensed with, medieval warfare was a gruesome business, and the author of the

AMA doesn't seek to spare us from the details. In the heat of these battles, and at the heart of the story, stands Arthur, King of Britain and indisputably the central character of this very English poem. By contrast, Lancelot has only a walk-on part, and Arthur is restored from his peripheral role in the French Romances to take centre stage. It is Arthur's fate which hangs in the balance, and if Arthur should fall then the Round Table and the country will fall with him; nothing less than the future of Britain is at stake. With Arthur's demise, the author seems to be telling us what we already know, that all things must come to pass, and on that level the poem is a solid reinforcement of the inevitability of change. But there is also a moral dimension to Arthur's fate, in which actions have their eventual consequences. When Arthur embarks on his military undertaking there is a sense of a wrong being righted, the prosecution of a war in the name of justice and honour. But when he struts about, god-like, on the walls of Metz without armour or shield we catch a glimpse of a man who has started to believe in his infallibility and immortality. As his forces push violently and without mercy into Tuscany and begin eying the bigger prize of Rome itself, personal glory appears to be the motive, coupled with boastfulness and pride, and it is at this moment that Fortune's Wheel must turn.

There are many challenges facing the translator of this poem. For all the candle-lit hours that the original scribe worked on what must have been a labour of love, certain words or even lines are, or have become, indecipherable, and a relative lack of punctuation leads to ambiguity and in some cases contradiction when trying to follow the progression of thought or the structure of an argument. Stock phrases and alliterative formulations are repeated again and again; to the medieval mind they might have provided a kind of reassuring continuity or even the glue by which the story hung together, but to the contemporary reader they often seem slack or unnecessary. For example, I can only assume that the soldiers of Genoa are 'giants' not because of some geo-specific DNA coding which enhanced their physical stature but because Genoa and giant happen to share the same consonant. The sheer number of characters is also a complication; some appear to have been created only for alliterative convenience, and some have very similar names despite fighting for different armies. The author of the manuscript obviously found the cast list somewhat confusing as well. At line 1433 Sir Berill appears to have died (at the very least he is 'borne down') in a Roman counter-attack, only to be found escorting the prisoner convoy at line 1605 and to be killed once more by the King of Libya in the Cutting of Clime, wherever that might be. Likewise, in the original, Sir Bedivere seems to have been buried first in Bayonne and then just a few lines later in Burgundy, just prior to Sir Cador being buried in Caen, only to be found standing at Arthur's side 2,000 lines later ready to ride into battle with Mordred. Even the Emperor Lucius isn't immune from this kind of apparent inconsistency. At lines 2076–9 he is speared by Lancelot, the lance entering his hip, passing through his stomach to protrude from his back by several inches, but by line 2220 he is fighting fit once again. I hesitate to say that these moments reflect lapses of concentration on behalf of the scribe since it is possible they have some deeper textual relevance, but rightly or wrongly I have tried to devise unobtrusive strategies to make sense of the most glaringly contradictory material, and I hope readers will forgive me my own errors of judgement where they have inevitably occurred. For reference, I have included a list of characters, and might well have attached an atlas of medieval Europe as well, though it has to be remembered that the *AMA* contains as many speculations about the 'real world' as it does about the world of fantasy, and that the original author's 'map' should not necessarily be used for navigational purposes.

Typically, each line of the original has four stresses, two falling either side of a caesura, and contains three alliterating syllables, usually two on the left side of the divide then one on the right, followed by an unalliterating stressed syllable, a pattern which might be represented by the equation xx/xy. So for example:

'I am comen fro the conquerour   courtais and gentle'
[987]

But other patterns exist within the poem, and some lines show no demonstrable alliteration at all, offering the contemporary translator a level of flexibility or leeway when it comes to re-engineering the poem's acoustics. It should also be noted that all vowels and the letter aitch share the same alliterative value in poems such as this, and I have happily followed suit. I have also attempted, where meaning and diction would allow, to imitate the original poet's habit of continuing the same alliteration over several lines, like a kind of knowingly extravagant riff. The practice is unusual and something of a trademark quality of the *AMA*; it gives us a sense of a poet revelling in the playfulness of language and not embarrassed by the range of his vocabulary.

The original is inconsistent in its use of section breaks or what we might loosely describe as verses, so to open the poem up and make it easier on the eye I have added my own breaks and indents where it seemed appropriate. And one further imposition: after much deliberation, I took the decision to present this translation entirely in the past tense, when the original fluctuates between past and historical present. The present tense clearly helps to activate and animate certain scenes, and I had assumed at one stage that its usage was reserved for moments of high drama and close combat. But repeated reading of the poem reveals no such consistency of approach. In fact there are occasions when the poem switches tense within the same passage, within the same sentence, sometimes within the same line, and if there is an underlying pattern or a good reason for such variation, it has eluded me. It is possible that here and there I have sacrificed some of the urgency and emotion of the original for the sake of a smooth read and to comply with modern grammatical expectations, but at the very outset the speaker in the poem assumes the role of narrator, inviting us to gather round and listen to a 'tale', i.e. something that happened in the past, and I have continued in that storytelling mode.

I have used Larry D. Benson's (1974) transcription and annotations as a foundation text for this translation, with reference as well to critical editions by Mary Hamel (1984) and Valerie Krishna (1976). No transcription agrees entirely with another on the meaning of words and phrases, and even the total number of lines in the poem is a matter of debate. Surrounded by such dedicated scholarship and research, I have not been in a position to judge the rights and wrongs of particular arguments, and on occasions, when faced with problems of interpretation, I have had to fall back on a sense of tonal consistency or simply trust my own poetic inclinations. Valerie Krishna's *New Verse Translation* (1983) and the translation by Brian Stone for

Penguin Classics (1988) have been essential reading, and two other indispensable publications were *The Cambridge Companion to the Arthurian Legend* (ed. Archibald and Putter, 2009) and *Arthurian Studies ii, The Alliterative Morte Arthure* (ed. Göller, 1994). Huge thanks go to Professor James Simpson of Harvard University for his advice and wisdom and for his scrupulous overseeing of this translation.

So did King Arthur exist? There are no bones, no crowns, no credible documents and no archaeological evidence of any type whatsoever to say that he did, and those geographical sites across Britain which claim some connection with his birth, his life or his death are either those of legend and fancy or tourist destinations conceived by the heritage industry or avaricious monks. True, some modern scholarship points to a set of circumstances in which Arthur might have operated as a leader in battle, not in the south or west but in the north of England between York and Hadrian's Wall, but it is little more than a vacancy which an Arthur-size figure might have occupied, or conditions in which someone like Arthur could have existed and succeeded. It makes Arthur a possibility, and even if those odds are increased to a probability, we would still need to strip away the fantasy and the anachronisms before we could even begin to consider him as a genuine inhabitant of sixth-century Britain. On the other hand, King Arthur lives on in the imagination perhaps as strongly as he ever did, and not just in literature but as a star of screen and stage and in many forms of popular culture and high art. No matter how many times he receives his death blow and is carried to Glastonbury or ferried to Avalon, Arthur remounts and rides again. It is also interesting to note how adaptable and available Arthur has been, from the first whisperings right up to the present day, flying the flag for whoever has needed or embraced him, be it the Welsh, the Celts, the Normans, the French, the British, the Cornish or the English. In that sense, all those claims which describe Arthur as 'The once and future king' have yet to be disproved.

SIMON ARMITAGE

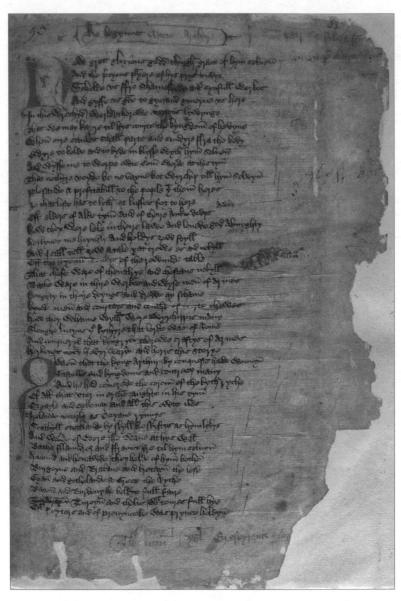

Opening lines of the manuscript of the *Alliterative Morte Arthure*
(Thornton Manuscript, Lincoln Cathedral MS. 91)

The Death of King Arthur

The Death of King Arthur

*Here begins the Death of Arthur. In the name of the Father,
the Son and the Holy Spirit. Amen for Charity. Amen.*

~

N ow may God, great and glorious, by His very grace
and the precious prayers of His perfect mother,
shield us from shame and sinful deeds,
and through His grace may we guide and be governed
in this wretched world, so by virtuous ways
we may come to His court, the kingdom of heaven,
where our soul and body shall sever their bond
and abide there by Him in bliss for ever;
and may words trip from my tongue at this time,
not hollow and vain but in honour of Him,
and which profit and please every person who hears them.

You who are listeners and love to learn
of the heroes of history and their awesome adventures
who were loyal to the law and loved Almighty God,
come closer and heed me; hold yourselves quiet
and I'll tell you a tale both noble and true

The poet introduces the poem

of the royal ranks of the Round Table
who were champion knights and chivalrous chieftains,
both worldly wise and brave in battle,
daring in their deeds, always dreading shame,
kind, courteous men, courtly in their manners.
How they won in war the worship of many,
who ripped life from wicked Lucius, the Lord of Rome
and conquered that kingdom through the art of combat . . .
Attend with your ears as this tale is told!

King Arthur had at length acquired by conquest
many castles, kingdoms and countless regions
and recovered the crown of all those countries
once owned by Uther in his earthly days:
Argyll, Orkney and the outer isles,
the whole of Ireland, hemmed in by the Ocean,
malevolent Scotland to lead as he liked,
Wales, which he took at will through warfare,
Flanders and France, which were his for free,
Holland and Hainault, both of which he held,
Burgundy and Brabant and also Brittany,
Guyenne, Gotland and magnificent Grasse,
Bayonne and Bordeaux where he built so beautifully
and Touraine and Toulouse with their lofty towers.
They declared him Prince of Poitiers and Provence,
of Valence and Vienne, so high in value,
of Anjou and Auvergne, prosperous earldoms;
after crushing conquests they saluted him as Sovereign
of Navarre and Normandy and also Norway,
and of Austria and Germany and umpteen others;

A summary of Arthur's conquests

Denmark he suppressed through the power of his person,
and from Sluys to Sweden with a swish of his sword.

    When these deeds were done he dubbed his knights
and dealt out dukedoms in different lands,
anointing his relatives as royal rulers
of the countries whose crowns they coveted the most.
Then as ruler of those peoples in the realms he had ridden,
the rightful King rested, convened the Round Table,
and spent that season perusing his own pleasure
in the heartlands of Britain, which he liked the best,
then went west into Wales with his warring companions
and swung to the south with his swiftest hounds
to hunt down his deer through those high hills.
In Glamorgan gladness was as great as anywhere,
and with his lords' assent he constructed a city
of well-built walls which they called Caerleon
on the banks of the beautiful river which runs there,
where his army might assemble should he summon them to arms.

    For the Christmas season he was seated at Carlisle,
that celebrated Sovereign, asserting his majesty
over dukes and the like from distant lands,
over earls and archbishops and others of their ilk,
and bishops, and knights whether bannered or not,
who would follow his flag wherever it flew.
On Christmas Day, when the crowd were all gathered,
the conquering King gave his guests a command
that no lord should so much as mention leaving
until ten days of feasting were fully taken.

Christmas at Carlisle with the Round Table

So in royal array the Round Table was hosted,
amid splendid entertainment and extravagant cuisine,
and in human history never was such nobleness
witnessed in mid-winter in those western marches.

But on New Year's Day, on the stroke of noon,
as bread was being brought to bold men at the table,
a senator of Rome appeared suddenly in their presence,
with sixteen knights standing in his shadow.
He saluted the Sovereign and those seated in hall,
inclining respectfully to king after king
and greeting Queen Guinevere as courtesy required.
Then, bowing to Arthur, he embarked on his business:
'Sir Lucius Iberius, Emperor of Rome,
salutes you as his subject, under imperial seal;
this statement is worded with stern instruction –
his sign is its truth, so treat it as no trifle.
Now on New Year's Day, signed by a notary,
I serve you this summons to sue for your lands,
so on Lammas Day, without detour or delay,
be ready in Rome with your Round Table
to appear in his presence with your princely knights,
just as daylight dawns, on pain of death,
in the famous Capitol, before the true King,
where he sits with his senate in the style that suits them,
to answer what he asks of you: why you occupy his lands
that owe homage of old to his ancestral elders,
and why you have robbed and ransacked and ransomed
and killed his kinsmen who are royal kings.
You are called to account for the actions of your company

Messengers arrive from Rome

who are rebels to Rome and default on its revenues.
If this summons is snubbed, he sends you this warning:
he shall seek you overseas with sixteen kings
and burn Britain to oblivion and obliterate your knights,
and leash you like the tamest beast that ever breathed;
you shall sleep not one wink under watching skies
though you hide in a hole being hunted by Rome.
For if you flee into France or Friesland or further
our forces shall fetch you and finish you forever.
We find in our records that your father paid fealty
to the registry of Rome, and rightly so.
No more trifling. You are told we seek tribute
won by Julius Caesar and the soldiers who served him.'

      The King fixed the foreigner with a fearsome stare,
the anger in his eyes like glowing embers.
His face became flushed with the fire of fury
till he looked like a lion, and he bit his lip.
And those Romans fell to the floor in fear,
appalled by his expression, expecting the end.
They cowered like pups in the presence of the King –
they seemed utterly alarmed by his looks alone.
Then one knight, from his knees, pleaded imploringly:
'Most natural of kings, courteous and noble,
for your honour's sake spare us emissaries from harm;
since power here is your privilege we appeal for mercy.
We are ruled by Sir Lucius, Lord of all Rome,
the most marvellous man in the width of the world,
and to do as he likes is our loyal duty.
We come at his command, so have us excused.'

                                        A summons is served

  Then the Sovereign spoke and his words were scathing.
'Ha! Craven knight, what a creeping coward.
If one knight standing near were annoyed in the slightest
you'd be loath for all Lombardy to look at him once.'
'Sir,' said the senator, 'as Christ is my saviour,
the cruelty in your eyes has cut us to the core.
Of the lords I have looked on, you are the lordliest.
I speak no lie – your stare is lion-like.'
'You have summoned me, and your statement is spoken;
for your leader's sake I shall suffer you still longer.
Since my head was anointed with holy oil
no beast ever blustered so brazenly before me.
But with holy kings I shall hold council,
and dukes and nobles and doctors of degree,
and peers of the parliament and also prelates,
and the esteemed ranks of the Round Table.
Valuable advice from the valiant I shall seek,
and shall work by the wit of my wise knights.
Now, to waste further breath would find me unworthy,
as would reaping revenge in a frenzied rage.
You shall lodge here, therefore, with these loyal lords,
for seven nights be hosted and shall stable your horses,
and see life as we live it in these humble lands.'

  Respectful of Rome, which was ever the richest,
he commanded Sir Kay, 'Take care of these lords,
serve them to the standards their status insists,
and make haste to house them in the choicest chambers,
then show them to the hall to be seated and served.
What they hope for they shall have, be it hay for their horses

Arthur's response

or wine or wax candles or all of earth's wealth.
Spare no spices and spend without stint,
the breadth of abundance shall know no boundary.
Uphold my honour, sir, and hand on heart
you shall be wealthily rewarded, and never go without.'

So they are harboured in court and hosted most highly,
welcomed warmly by the knights within those walls.
In their chambers by firelight they changed their clothes,
then a chancellor escorted them with all due ceremony.
Soon the senator was seated, as his status demanded,
at the King's top table, with two knights in attendance,
by himself, singly, as Arthur would be served,
like royalty, from the right, at the Round Table.
For the Romans, in their reign, were regarded greatly,
and their blood was as royal as any on earth.

The first course was carried in before the King in person,
boars' heads strewn with sparkling silver
served by smartly dressed, highly skilled men
of noble descent, sixty in number.
Then came flesh that for a season had fattened on frumenty,
plus beasts of all manner and many a grand bird,
peacocks and plovers on golden platters,
porcupined piglets which had never known pasture,
herons half hidden in their own fine feathers,
plump swans presented on silver plates,
Turkish tartlets to tantalise the tongue,
meat in pastry that would melt in the mouth,
shoulder of boar, the best meat served sliced,

9   *A feast is prepared*

bakings of bitterns and barnacle geese,
young hawks in bread, not easy to better,
and belly pork that bubbled juicily on the plate.
Then steaming stews to delight and satisfy,
in azure sauce, so they seemed to be aflame.
And fire appeared to flare from each slice of flesh
that all lords who looked upon it would love.
Then cranes and curlews cannily roasted,
rabbit meat coloured by the cream sauce it came in,
and pheasant which flashed with silver flourishings.
and dozens of dainty decorated pastries.

Then came claret and Cretan wines cunningly decanted
through a system of pipes made of pure silver,
wines of Alsace and Iberia and others of that ilk,
of the Rhine and Rochelle which are reckoned the richest,
and valued white wines from the vines of Venice
from fine gold taps to tempt their taste-buds.

In the King's own cabinet, covered with silver,
gilded goblets gave a golden glow;
there was a chief steward, a chevalier of some standing,
courteous Sir Kay who would charge the cups,
and the Sovereign possessed sixty, a matching set
exquisitely crafted, intricately carved,
every part being studded with precious stones
so no poison could be secretly slipped inside
or the blend would blast the bright gold to bits
or the virtue of the gems would make void the venom.
The Sovereign himself was resplendently arrayed,

The feast is served

robed in rich gold, surrounded by his knights,
adorned in his diadem on the high dais,
being deemed the most dignified that dwelt on earth.

Then the conquering King spoke politely to those lords,
put the Romans at rest with his royal words:
'Sirs, be bold in your manner and brighter in your mood;
we know nothing in this country of notable cuisine,
for in this barren land of Britain no game is bred,
so force down the food without doling out false praise,
and fill up on poor fare, which you find before you.'
'Sir,' said the senator, 'as Christ will save me,
within Rome's walls never reigned such royalty.
Any prelate or pope or prince in this world
would be happy to eat such an excellent meal.'

Then in order of worthiness they washed and went
hall-wards,
the conquering King and his noble knights,
Guinevere with good Sir Gawain to one side,
and Sir Uhtred on the other, Overlord of Turin.
Then spices were served with no expense spared,
then malmsey and muscatel, both marvellous wines,
went rapidly around in ruby red cups
to each and all, be they Roman or otherwise.
Then the courteous King, since he cared to do so,
assigned to the senator some stalwart lords
to lead him to his chamber when he chose to leave,
among the mirth and merriment of gracious minstrelsy.

The feasting comes to a close

Then the Conqueror, in due course, went into council
with his lords and liegemen who were loyal to his cause;
to the Giant's Tower he went in good temper
with his generals and judges and just knights.
Sir Cador of Cornwall addressed the King
with a pleasing expression and warmth in his words.
'For the trouble that threatens I thank God thoroughly.
You'll be trapped by this treachery, unless you trick better.
This letter from Sir Lucius makes my heart laugh!
We have lived at our leisure now for many long days,
capering as we please through all points of the compass
till the fame that we fought for has frittered away.
I blush, by our lord, for our best baronage
whom we painfully disappoint by our abuse of power.
Now war has awoken – may Christ be worshipped!
May valour and vigour bring us victory again!'

'Sir Cador, you counsel is noble,' said the King,
You're a marvellous man of merry words.
But you take no account of the case or its consequences,
simply hurling from your head what happens in your heart.
We must tease out the truths and proceed tactfully,
giving talk to this topic which troubles my heart.
You see that the Emperor is certainly angered,
from his messengers it seems he is mightily dismayed.
His senator has summoned me and spoken at will,
behaved hideously in my hall with hateful words,
slurring and slandering and sparing me no shame.
I could hardly answer, for my heart shook with anger.
Like a tyrant he told me to pay tribute to Rome,

Arthur holds council in the Giant's Tower

so sadly conceded by our conquering forebears
when foreigners, in the absence of armed defences,
claimed it from our commonwealth, so the chronicles say.
In truth, it is Rome that owes tribute to me!
For my ancestors were Emperors and owned it outright;
Belinus and Brennius and Baldwin the Third
occupied the empire for eight score winters,
each inheriting it in turn, as the old men tell.
They won the Capitol and sent its walls crashing,
and hanged their head men a hundred at a time.
Then our kinsman Constantine was its next conqueror
who was heir to all England and a Roman Emperor,
and by armed combat captured the cross
on which Christ the Heavenly King was crucified;
on which evidence we ask the Emperor to explain
by what right those who reign in Rome make their claim.'

        Then King Angus spoke, giving answer to Arthur.
'You ought to be overlord above every authority,
you are wisest and worthiest and the mightiest warrior,
and most kingly of counsel that ever wore the crown.
I speak for Scotland, and we suffered from their skirmishing;
while the Romans reigned here they ransomed our nobles
and ran riot through the regions, raping our wives,
robbing us blind without reason or right.
So I shall swear an oath to our Saviour in heaven
and devoutly make a vow to the vernicle most virtuous,
that vengeance shall visit this great villainy
when my valiant knights vie with venomous men.
I shall find you the finest of fighting forces,

King Angus of Scotland swears his loyalty

twenty thousand men within two months
to deploy as you please, paid from my pocket,
to attack those foes who would treat us without favour.'

   Then the burly Baron of Brittany, a bold man,
gave opinion to Arthur, politely imploring
to answer those aliens with hard-hitting words
and rile the Romans till they rode through the mountains,
saying, 'Verily I make a vow to my Messiah
and the holy vernicle, that I shall hold hard
in the face of all Romans who reign in any realm,
and am rigged out ready and waiting for war,
less worried by the forceful wielding of their weapons
than by damp dew as it drifts downwards,
less bothered by the swing of their sharp swords
than by fair flowers that spring from the fields.
Battle-hungry men I shall bring into the breach,
thirty thousand in total, all armed to the teeth,
in a month and no more, to march at your word,
and to deploy in any province just as you please.'

   'Ah ah!' said the Welsh King, 'and worshipped be Christ!
Now the agony of our ancestors shall be answered with vengeance.
In the west of Wales such atrocity they wrought
just to think of that war causes weeping and woe.
I shall have the vanguard, and have it as my own
till that rogue the Viscount of Rome is routed
who wronged me once, did me villainy at Viterbo
as I passed in pilgrimage through Pontremoli.
Being in Tuscany at the time he took my men,

14   *Pledges of support from Brittany and Wales*

arrested them without right then held them for ransom.
I promise him now no peaceful appeasement
till fortune finds us face to face
and we deal out our dreadful blows to the death.
From my purse I shall pay for princely knights,
the most mighty from Wales and the Western Marches,
two thousand all told, sitting tall in the saddle,
the most weapon-ready warriors in the western lands.'

    Sir Ewain Fitz Urien then made urgent inquiry,
a kinsman of the Conqueror and himself courageous:
'Make us privy, sir, to your plans and we shall put them into practice;
whether adjourn for a while or journey now to war:
to ride against Rome and ravage their land
we would ready our soldiery to sail at your say-so.'

    'Comrade,' said the King, 'you kindly enquire
if my counsel accords to the conquest of those lands.
By the first of June we shall fully engage them
with the cruellest of knights, so help me Christ.
To my Saviour, therefore, I do solemnly swear,
and make a vow to the vernicle, wholly virtuous:
at Lammas I shall leave and linger as I choose
in Lorraine or Lombardy just as I like,
then move on to Milan and undermine the walls
of Pietrasanta and Pisa and Pontremoli.
In the Vale of Viterbo my knights shall find victual,
and with their sovereign shall enjoy a six-week sojourn,
while riders will be sent to besiege the city
unless terms of a treatise be offered in that time.'

Arthur vows to fight

'For certain,' said Sir Ewain, 'I swear the same:
should I ever set eyes on the man that you mention
who occupies your heritage – the Empire of Rome –
I shall risk all to rip down that eagle
which is borne on his banner of brightest gold,
wrestle it from his retinue and rive it to pieces
unless rough-minded knights rush in for its rescue.
In the field I will supply you with fresh reinforcements,
fifty thousand of the finest on thoroughbreds,
to descend on your foe as you find fitting,
in France or in Friesland, fighting as you choose.'

'By my Lord,' said Sir Lancelot, 'now lightens my heart.
I thank God for the loyalty these lords have given.
Let lesser men have leave to speak as they like
without tying their tongues, but I tell you this:
I shall fight from the first with my fellow knights;
on my quick-footed steed, copiously equipped,
I'll brawl with Sir Lucius before battle is launched,
joust as his giants and Genoans stand by,
swiftly strike him from his steed by the strength of my hand
right under the eyes of the army that aids him.
Once my retinue is arrayed, I rate it straightforward
to rush into Rome with rampaging knights.
Within seven nights, with six score of soldiers
you shall find me at sea, ready to set sail.'

Then Sir Lot laughed and spoke out loudly,
'I like it that Sir Lucius longs for such sorrow;
since war is what he wants, his worries now begin;

Arthur's knights rise to the challenge

our work is to wreak the wrath of our fathers.
I vow to God and the virtuous vernicle:
should I meet those Romans who are reckoned so mighty,
arrayed in their ranks in battle's arena,
I would readily, for the reverence of the Round Table,
ride in and rout them, frontline and rearguard,
slash swathes with my sword for my allies to swarm through
and where my steed rushes so red blood shall run.
He that follows behind and is first in the aftermath
will find in my footsteps many fallen to their death.'

And the Sovereign solemnly saluted those knights,
praised them greatly for their pledges of support.
'May our God in heaven honour you all;
as long as I lead you may I never lose you.
My title and name you maintain across nations
and uphold my honour in alien kingdoms;
you have won me my wealth and my worth through this world
and the claims of my crown were secured by your courage.
He whose fellows are such friends need fear no foe,
but is free to take force to whatever front he likes.
No king under Christ will I fear or kowtow to
while you stand at my side. Your strength is my all.'

After talking in trust, a trumpet sounded
and they dutifully came down, dukes and earls
to assemble in the hall and swiftly take supper,
this gathering of the good with their grace and their splendour.
Then the mighty monarch amused his men
with uproarious entertainment for the whole Round Table

17   *Arthur salutes his comrades*

for seven full days, till the senator insisted,
with unsubtle speech, on an answer for his Emperor.

Once Epiphany had past, when all points had been raised
by peers of the parliament, prelates and others,
the courteous King in his council chamber
summoned the strangers and spoke with them personally.
'Give greeting to lord Lucius, but allow for no illusion:
if you follow him faithfully then inform him at once
that I leave at Lammas and shall set up lodge
and take leisure in his lands with my fellow lords,
like the ruler of that realm, taking rest as I please;
then by the River Rhone call together my Round Table,
and confiscate assets all across the countryside,
no matter how mighty and menacing he might be.
Then will I move through the mountains and march on his
    heartlands,
to marvellous Milan to wallop down its walls.
In Lorraine and Lombardy I shall leave not one man
who lives by his laws or is loyal to his cause,
then turn into Tuscany at a time that suits me
and ransack wide regions with my riotous knights.
Bid him hurry to salvage some scrap of his honour
and meet me on the plains if he prizes his pride.
He will find me in France, let him hunt me as he fancies,
from the first of February in those foreign fields;
before forfeiting any land or falling to his forces
the flower of his folk shall be ploughed into the furrow.
I swear, with all certainty, by the sign of my seal,
to besiege Rome's citadel within seven winters

Arthur's reply to the Romans

and so strictly encircle it from every side
that many senators will sigh at the sound of my name.
My summons is signed and served to you, Sir,
with a promise of safe passage. You may leave when you please.
I shall plan your journey, plot it out personally,
form this place to the port where you put out to sea.
Seven days to Sandwich and not a second more:
sixty miles a day – the distance should not daunt you.
You must strike with the spurs never sparing the steeds,
going straight by Watling Street and no other way.
Dismount for the day where dusk comes to meet you
be it forest or field, and not one foot further,
then bind your horses to a branch by the bridle
and lodge by a lime tree in what comfort you can.
No foreigner will be found moving furtively at night
with such a callous crew as accompanies yourselves.
The limit of your licence is witnessed by these lords:
fair or unfair, however you find it,
your life and your limb hang by its every letter,
though Lucius has risked on this the lordship of Rome.
Should you still be found standing within our strandline
on the eighteenth day when the dawn bell tolls,
hurtling horses will tear you into hundredths
and hungry hounds will gnaw you where you hang,
and all the red gold and the riches of Rome
will be found insufficient to fund your ransom.'

    'Sir,' said the senator, 'so Christ save me,
should I pass from this place with my pride still intact,
for no other Emperor that exists upon earth

Roman delegation promised safe passage

will I come to Arthur on an errand such as ours.
But I stand here, just myself and my sixteen knights –
I beseech you, sir, to assure our safety;
if some lawless person should impede our progress
and you licence it, lord, then your honour is lost.'
'Fear not,' said the King, 'your conduct is secured
from Carlisle to the coast where your ships will cast off.
If the coffers on your crafts were crammed with silver
my seal would still bring safety for sixty miles further.'

They paid kindness to the King and requested their leave.
With Carlisle behind them, riding hard on their horses,
courteous Sir Cador set them on their course,
escorting them to Catterick then commending them to Christ.
They struck with their spurs till their steeds were shattered,
then hurriedly hired fresh horses in their place,
riding in fear and not flagging or resting
except to lie beneath a lime when daylight lapsed.
And the senator never strayed from the straightest route.
Before the seventh day ceased they had reached the city,
and never under heaven were they happier to hear
the sound of the sea and the bells of Sandwich.
Without stalling, the steeds were stabled on board;
wearily to the pallid water they went.
They helped their sailors to heave up the anchor
and fled at high flood. To Flanders they rowed,
then went fast through its fields, as fitted their cause,
then to Aachen in Germany, still in Arthur's ownership.
They went by Mount St Gothard and its grievous passes
and across the lowlands of lovely Lombardy,

The Romans make a hasty return

turning into Tuscany with its turrets and high towers,
and presently they changed into precious apparel.
By Sunday, in Sutri, they rested their steeds,
and by assent of all knights sought the saints of Rome.
Then they spurred to the palace with its superb portal
where Sir Lucius was lodged with many of his lords,
bowing low their heads as they handed over
the sealed missive with its solemn message.

        The Emperor was eager and urgent with enquiry,
asking what answers Arthur had given,
how he rules his subjects, the realms he reigns in,
if he rises against Rome, and the rights that he claims.
'You should have seized his sceptre and asserted your high
        status
for the reverence and respect of royal Rome;
you were sent in my service as my special envoi –
for honour's sake he should have served you himself!'

        'That he wouldn't, for any one in the width of the world,
except the man who defeats him by military might.
Many fellows shall lie felled on the field of battle
before this place sees his presence, despite all pressure.
I say, Sir, that Arthur is your enemy forever,
and has eyes to be overlord of the whole Roman Empire
which was owned by his ancestors except for Uther.
At New Year I myself announced your notice
to that noble of great name and before his nine kings,
in the most regal surroundings of the Round Table.
I delivered the summons as his lords looked on,

The messengers arrive in Rome

and in faith, such fear I never once felt
in all the princes' palaces I have passed through in life.
I would surrender my status and Roman stalwarts
before meeting that monarch with a message once more.
He may be chosen the chief among all other chieftains,
both by eminence in combat and elegant conduct,
the worthiest, the wisest and most muscular in warfare
of the millions of men I have met with in this world,
the knightliest creature that Christendom has known
amongst kings or conquerors crowned upon earth;
of bearing, of boldness, of brutal expression
the most chivalrous knight to ever come beneath Christ.
If we speak of his spending he despises silver,
and rates gold no greater than a lump of granite,
and wine no better than water from the well,
and all the wealth in the world no match for worthiness.
In all countries of merit, no courtesies come close
to those kept by that King in his royal court.
I counted this Christmastime the anointed kings
to be ten at the table, with himself in the total.
Be warned and be wary, for war is his will;
pay a wage to many warriors to watch your borders
and to move with all might at a moment's notice,
for if he reaches into Rome he will rule it forever.
I propose that you prepare and postpone things no longer.
Have trust in your mercenaries and march them to the
    mountains;
while the year is young, if his health remains hearty,
he will stride this way with speed and with strength.'

22   *Arthur's reply is delivered to the Emperor*

'By Easter,' said the Emperor, 'I aim myself
to be garrisoned in Germany with gallant knights,
then push forward into France, that flower among kingdoms,
to find him and force him to forfeit his lands.
I shall send in scouts, shrewd and steadfast,
many giants from Genoa, masterful jousters,
to meet him in the mountains and martyr his men,
ambush them in passes and annihilate them forever.
On St Gothard we will set up a great watchtower,
guarded from harm by good men at arms,
with a beacon above it to burn if required,
so no armed enemy shall enter those mountains;
and a second shall be built at St Bernard's pass,
bolstered by bannerets and bachelor knights.
Through the gates of Pavia no prince shall pass,
or through places made perilous by my prize men.'

Then Sir Lucius despatched lordly letters:
to the Orient, carried there by courageous couriers,
to Ambyganye and Orcage and Alexandria also,
to India and Armenia by the flowing Euphrates,
to Asia and Africa and all of Europe,
to Hyrcania and Elam and those distant outposts,
to Arabia and Egypt and to every leader
who occupied land in those eastern empires
of Damascus and Damietta, all dukes and earls.
And in dread of his displeasure they prepared without delay.
From Crete and Cappadocia many noble kings
came and came quickly, minding his command.
Towards Tartary and Turkey, after hearing the tidings,

Lucius declares war

they travelled via Thebes, powerful tyrants,
and the flower of the folk of the Amazon came flowing;
those who failed to take the field were forfeited forever.
From Babylon and Baghdad came the boldest men,
knights and their knaves, waiting no more.
From Persia and Pamphilia and the lands of Prester John
every Prince who held power prepared a force;
the Sultan of Syria assembled his soldiers
from the Nile to Nazareth in huge numbers;
from Gadara to Galilee they quickly grouped,
all the sultans of states who were servants to Rome.
They gathered by the Greek Sea with their grievous weapons,
in their great galleys with glittering shields.
The Cypriot King waited on the water for the Sultan
with the royal ranks of Rhodes arrayed all around him,
then they sailed in strong winds over the salty waves,
swiftly, those Saracens, seizing the moment.
And accordingly all those kings arrived at Corneto,
a sixty-mile ride from the city of Rome.
By now the Greeks had gathered in great strength,
Macedonia's mightiest and men of those marches,
and Apulians and Prussians pressing on with the rest,
the liegemen of Lithuania with scores of legions.
Thus the squadrons arrived, all of them sizable,
assorted Saracens from several lands,
the Sultan of Syria and sixteen kings,
assembling at the soonest in the city of Rome.

Then the Emperor entered, extravagantly armed,
arrayed with his Romans on their royal mounts,

Rome's military allies assemble

sixty giants in front, engendered by fiends,
with witches and warlocks to watch his tents
whichever way he went, in winter, through the years.
No horse could hold them, those hulking churls,
so chain-mail-covered camels carried them on towers.
He set out with those aliens in a huge army,
journeyed into Germany which was judged to be Arthur's,
rode along the river in a riotous manner,
and took pleasure in the plundering of those prized places.

     A war in Westphalia he won with ease,
then drew in by the Danube and dubbed his new knights.
In the countryside of Cologne he besieged castles,
and sojourned that season with Saracens by the score.

     On day eight of St Hilary, King Arthur himself
in his honoured council gave orders to his lords:
'Return to your territories and rally your troops
and meet me at Cotentin, mightily equipped.
Await me at Barfleur on those welcoming waters
going boldly aboard with the best of your men;
I shall faithfully join you in those far-flung fields.'
Swiftly he sent out his sergeants-at-arms
to command all his mariners to marshal ships,
and within sixteen days his fleet was assembled
on the sea at Sandwich to sail at his order.
In the Palace of York he convened a parliament
for all peers of the realm, prelates and such persons,
and in the presence of lords, when prayers had passed,
the King in his council declared these words:

Arthur convenes his forces

'Along perilous roads I propose now to pass,
conquering those countries with my keen men,
and outfoxing my enemies, should fortune be fair,
who occupy my heritage – the Empire of Rome.
I assign to you a sovereign, should you show your assent:
my sister's own son, Sir Mordred himself,
shall be left here to rule, lord lieutenant
over all loyal liegemen in my lands who have lordship.'
Then he called to that kinsman, himself in the council:
'Sir knight, I name you as keeper of my kingdoms,
a rightful warden to rule over these realms
I have won in war across this wide world.
See that Guinevere, my wife, be worthily regarded
so her heart's desire be hers for the asking,
and grant my great castles be grandly equipped
should she choose to hold court there in chivalrous company.
Defend my fine forests, or our friendship falters,
and let Guinevere and no other hunt the hills and hollows,
though only in season, when the game are good with grease-fat,
so her sport shall be taken at the stated time.
Change as you please any chancellors and chamberlains;
auditors and officers – ordain them yourself,
so too jurors and judges, justices of the peace,
and do right when dealing with those who do wrong.
If our Deity decrees that death is my destiny
I appoint you executor with exclusive power
to apportion my possessions for my soul's salvation
among mendicants and those fallen into miserable mischief.
Take heed of the huge total of my hoard of treasure
which I trust to you entirely – betray me never.

Arthur entrusts his kingdom to Mordred

As you will ultimately answer to the Almighty Judge
whose will in this world is enacted as he wishes,
be true in faithfully fulfilling my testament.
I pass to you completely all the power of my crown,
all my worldly wealth and my wife as well;
be faultless in your deeds so no offence be found
when I land again in my country, if Christ should allow me.
If you have in you the grace to govern with goodness
I shall crown you, my knight, a king with my hands.'

Then Sir Mordred himself spoke most softly,
knelt low before his lord and delivered these words:
'I beseech you, sir, my sibling by blood,
that you choose another, in the name of charity.
In placing me in this plight you deceive your people,
my power being too simple for such a princely estate.
When others wise in warfare are worshipped hereafter
then I, in all honesty, will hardly be noticed.
To travel with your army is my true intention;
to support my prized knights I am packed and prepared.'

'You are my nearest nephew, nurtured from birth,
both cherished and chided like a child of my chamber.
Our bloodline is our bond, do not break from this duty.
You are aware what it means to work against my will.'

He swept out alone, lingered no longer
with the lords and liegemen who were left behind.
Then the conquering King went to his chamber
to give solace to the queen who was sitting in sorrow.

Mordred's protests are dismissed

Guinevere cried quietly, weeping as she kissed him,
and talked to him tenderly as her tears fell.
'I curse the man who caused this conflict,
who denies my heart of my honoured husband.
All the love in my life now marches from the land
and I am left alone and empty, believe me, forever.
Why not die, my dear love, die in your arms
before enduring the dread of this destiny on my own.'
'Guinevere, do not grieve, for the love of heavenly God.
Do not grudge my going, because good will follow.
Your unhappiness and weeping is wounding to my heart,
all the wealth of the world cannot wish away this woe.
I have named a noble knight to act as your guardian,
overlord of England, answerable to you only,
and that person is Sir Mordred, whom you have praised
    repeatedly,
a deputy, my dear, to attend your every desire.'
Then the lord took leave of the ladies in waiting,
kissed them and commended them to Christ's keeping.
Then she suddenly swooned as he called for his sword,
and fainted to the floor, as if death had undone her.
He hurried past his men and headed for his horse,
spurred from the palace with his special knights,
those royal riders of the Round Table,
speeding towards Sandwich. She saw him no more.

      There the great were gathered with gallant allies,
massing on the foreshore, fitted out marvellously.
Dukes and statesmen, some strutting on their steeds,
Earls of England, armies of archers,

Arthur's farewell to Guinevere

stout sheriffs shouting sharp instructions
to the troops who rallied before the Round Table,
assigning soldiers to certain lords
on the seafront, in the south, to sail at his say-so.
The barges being ready they rowed to the beach
to ferry aboard horses and fine battle-helmets,
loading the livestock in their livery and tack,
then the tents, the tough shields, tools to lay siege,
canopies, kit bags, exquisite coffers,
ponies, hackneys, horses-of-armour . . .
Thus the stuff of stern knights was safely stored.
And when all stock was stowed they stalled no longer,
timing their untying with the turn of the tide;
ships of all sizes ran up their sails,
all unfurling at the moment of their monarch's command,
and hands at the gunwales hauled up the great anchors,
watermen wise to the ways of the waves.
The crew at the bow began coiling in the cables
of the carriers and cutters and Flemish crafts;
they drew sails to the top, they tended the tiller,
they stood along the starboard singing their shanties.
The port's proudest ships found plentiful depth
and surged at full sail into changeable seas.
Without anyone being hurt they hauled in the skiffs:
shipmates looked sharp to shutter the portholes
and tested depth by lowering lead from the luff.
They looked to the lodestar as daylight lessened,
reckoned a good route when mist rose around them,
used their knowing with the needle-and-stone through the
    night,

The British set sail

when for dread of the dark they dropped their speed,
all the seadogs striking the sails at a stroke.

　　The Monarch was on his mighty boat with many men,
enclosed in a cabin among copious equipment.
And while resting on a richly arrayed bed
he was soothed to sleep by the swaying of the sea.
And he dreamed of a dragon dreadful to behold
that came darting over the deep to drown his people,
arrowing directly from the regions of the west
and swooping with menace over the sea's wide span.
His head and neck were hooded all over
with hazy azure, enamelled in bright hues.
His shoulders were shawled in shining silver
so the serpent was shielded by steely scales.
His wings and his womb were wondrously coloured
and in his marvellous mail he mounted the heavens.
His tail was tasselled with bladed tongues   [769A]
so what fellows it touched were fatally felled.
His feet were furred in the finest sable
and his cruel claws were encased in pure gold.   [771A]
So furious were the flames that flowed from his lips
that the sea itself seemed to seethe with fire.
Then out of the east, to oppose him head-on,
from above the clouds came a brutish black bear,
huge paws and pads on the pillars of his legs
with pinion-sharp claws, curved in appearance.
Hateful and hideous were his hairs and everything:
his legs were bandy and lagged with bushy bristles
all muddy and matted, and he foamed at the mouth,

Arthur's dream: the dragon and the bear

the foulest figure that was ever formed.
He went barrelling about with a bellicose look,
readying those raking claws for the clash.
He let rip with such a roar that the whole earth reeled,
striking out bloodily as he bullocked into battle.
Then the dragon in the distance dived straight for him,
and chased him through the sky with challenges and charges,
flying and fighting with the focus of a falcon.
He attacked with both fire and talons in tandem,
but the bear grew bigger and bolder in battle,
gouging flesh with his fearful fangs.
He caused such cuts with those cruel claws
that his breast and belly poured with blood,
and his blows were so crashing they cracked the earth's crust
and rivers ran red with crimson rain.
His strength alone might have laid low that lizard
were it not for the flames which he fired in defence.
The serpent ascended to the sky's ceiling,
then stooped steeply through the clouds and struck,
attacked with his talons and tore his back
which was ten foot in length from top to tail,
till the last living breath was beaten from that bear –
let him fall in the flood and float where it flows.
In his cabin, so disturbed was the King by those creatures
he nearly burst with the burden on the bed where he lay.

The King awoke, weary and weakened,
and two faithful philosophers who follow him were fetched,
sages in the subtleties of the seven sciences,
the cleverest clerics under Christ's heaven,

The dragon and the bear fight to the death

and he told them of his torment as he attempted to sleep.
'Haunted by those horrible, hulking beasts
my spirits are sapped. For the sake of God,
give meaning to my dream or I die this moment.'
'Sir,' said the sages, responding smartly,
'the dragon you dreamed of, so dreadful in appearance,
that came driving over the deep to drown your people,
is most certainly yourself, without a shadow of a doubt,
as you sail across the sea with your sound knights.
The colours which were cast so exquisitely on its wings
are the kingdoms of your crown which you lawfully conquered,
and the tattered tail with its long, trailing tongues
are the fine fellows who sail in your fleet.
The bear from above the clouds which was beaten
is a token of the tyrants making trouble for your people,
or some great giant you must grapple or joust with
and see off yourself in single combat.
You shall suffer no loss, if our Lord allow it,
but prevail to victory as your vision foretold.
So dread no longer this disturbing dream,
and care not, sir Conqueror, but comfort yourself
and those seamen who sail with your sturdy knights.'

At the sound of a trumpet they trimmed the sails
and rowed as one across the wide open waters.
They were fast in fording to the fine coast of Normandy;
at Barfleur the bold men on board were landed,
and found there a fleet of friends and followers,
the flower of all the folk of full fifteen realms,
for kings and captains had kept their appointment

Arthur's dream interpreted by sages

as Arthur had commanded at Christmas in Carlisle.
Once terrain had been reached and tents erected,
a Templar came at once seeking audience with Arthur:
'There is a monster near this mound tormenting your people,
a great giant of Genoa engendered by fiends.
He has gorged on the flesh of more than five hundred folk
and any number of babes of noble birth.
Such slaughter has sustained him over seven winters,
yet the sot is not sated, so much pleasure it serves him.
In the countryside near Cotentin no company has he spared
outside the keep of castles and their enclosing walls,
and has massacred many of the male offspring,
carrying them to his crag to pick their bones clean.
Just today he abducted the Duchess of Brittany
as she rode near to Rennes with her royal guards,
dragged her to the mountain where he makes his domain,
and will lie with that lady for as long as she lasts.
We followed from afar: we were five hundred strong,
barons and burghers and bachelors noble,
but he scaled his summit, and she screamed with such terror
in horror of that ogre . . . it will haunt me forever.
She was France's flower, and of all five realms
the fairest of the fair to be born by far,
judged the most genuine of jewels by just lords
from Genoa to Gironne, by Jesus in heaven.
She was kin to your Queen, as you're keenly aware,
of the highest royalty to reign on this earth.
As a proud King have pity on your people,
and avenge those victims so violated by that villain.'

Arthur learns of the monster of Mont St Michel

'Alas,' said Sir Arthur, 'to have lived so long!
Had word come of this, it would have worked out well.
The fate that befalls me is not fair but foul
now this fiend has defiled that fair lady.
France's fortune I would have forfeited for fifteen years
to have stood within a furlong and confronted that freak
as he snatched the heiress and hauled her to the hills.
I would sacrifice my own self before seeing her suffer.
So point me to the peak where he practises his torture;
I'll climb the crag and have my quarrel with that creature,
take the tyrant to task for his treason in these lands,
seek a truce until times and tidings are better.'

'Do you see, sir, that bluff where two bonfires burn?
There he lives and lurks, go there as you like,
to the crest of the crag by a cold well
which cascades down the cliffs with its clear streams.
You'll find there innumerable folk who are fallen,
and more florins, in faith, than France possesses,
and more stolen treasure taken by that traitor
than in all of Troy at the time it was toppled.'

Then the proud King cried out for pity of his people,
and lingered no longer, but strode to his lodgings.
There he writhed restlessly, wringing his hands,
and no person on this planet could imagine what he planned.
He called for Sir Kay, the bearer of his cup,
and bold Sir Bedivere, the bringer of his great sword.
'By evensong be armed to the hilt and on horseback
and meet by the bush where the brook runs brightly.

Arthur makes a secret plan

I propose to set out on a private pilgrimage
while the men are seated and being served their supper,
to seek out a saint by those salty streams
on Mount St Michael, where miracles have occurred.'

    So after evensong, Sir Arthur himself
went to his wardrobe and at once undid his clothes,
then dressed in a padded doublet with gold detail,
and over that a layer of Acre leather,
and on top of that a tunic of the choicest chain-mail,
then a sleeveless and scalloped surcoat of Jerodine.
On his head he pulled a helmet of highly polished silver,
Basle's very best, with vivid borders,
the crest and the coronal being beautifully enclosed
with clasps of costly gold encrusted with jewels.
The visor and face-guard were devoid of any defects,
stunningly enamelled and with silver-edged slits.
His gauntlets shone with gold and were edged at the hem
with seed pearls and stones of astounding tone.
He strapped on his broad shield, shouted for his bright
    sword,
strode to his brown steed and stood steadily on the ground
before stepping in the stirrup and swinging to the saddle,
reining him stoutly then steering him strongly,
spurring the brown steed as he sped to the bushes
where his men would meet him, mightily armed.
They rode by the river which ran most swiftly
where the branches overreached it beautifully from above.
Reindeer and roe bucked with reckless abandon
through rosebush and brake in a blissful riot.

        Arthur arms himself for combat

The forest flourished in the flush of many flowers,
with falcons and pheasants and their colours and fantails
and the flash of all fowls that fly on the wing,
and the cuckoo sang clearly from the copses and groves;
with gladness of all kinds they glory in their gifts.
The nightingale's notes made the sweetest noise;
three hundred of them had their say with the thrushes,
so the sound of streams and the singing of the birds
might soothe him whose soul had only known sorrow.
The fellows dismounted and pressed forward on foot,
haltering their horses at safe intervals.
Then the King gave a keen command to his knights
to stay by their steeds and to stray no further:
'I shall seek out this saint by myself alone,
have audience with the man who is master of this mountain,
and afterward make your offerings, one after the other,
to Saint Michael of this Mount, who is mighty with Christ.'

The King then clambered up the crag's steep cloughs,
climbing till he crested the brink of the cliff,
then lifted his visor and surveyed the view,
inhaling the coldness to keep himself calm.
He found the two fires with their fiercely burning flames
and forayed between them at a fourth of a furlong,
walked past the welling springs of water
to learn the whereabouts of that warlock's lair.
He forked to one fire, and right there he found
a woeful widow wringing her hands,
who was torn by grief and in tears, at a grave
dug out of the dirt as recently as midday.

Arthur scales the mount alone

He saluted that sad woman with words of sympathy,
and made careful enquires on the subject of the creature.

    The unhappy widow welcomed him and wept,
climbed to her knees and clasped her hands,
saying, 'Less sound, my sir, you speak too loudly.
If that beast hears you he'll butcher us both.
Curses on the scoundrel who stole your senses
and caused you to wander by these wild waters.
Honourably I tell you, it's horror that you aim for.
Why do you walk here, God-forsaken wanderer?
Do you hope to slay him with a slash of your sword?
A warrior even greater than Wade or Gawain
could win no worth here, I warn you in advance.
You've set about stalking this summit unsafely –
even six of your sort are too simple for his strength;
once you've clapped eyes on him you'll lack even the courage
to cross your heart, so hulking is that creature.
You seem noble and fair, in the first flush of knighthood,
but you are doomed to die, and that darkens my mood.
Were fifty such fellows to fight him in the field
the fist of that fiend would fell them as one.
Look, the dear Duchess, she was dragged here today,
lies dead and buried deep in the dust.
He murdered this mild one before midday was struck,
with no mercy in the world – it is meaningless to me.
He forced himself on her, defiled her, then finished her.
He slew her like a savage, slit her to the navel.
And here I have embalmed and buried her body;
in the wake of her hopelessness all my happiness is ended.

          A sad old woman cautions the King

Of her countless friends, none followed her footsteps,
only me, her foster-mother of fifteen winters.
I'll not strive to pass from this perilous promontory;
I'll be found in this field till the day of my fate.'

  Then Sir Arthur answered the old woman:
'I have come from the Conqueror, courteous and honourable,
as one of the hardest of Arthur's knights,
a messenger to this muck-heap, bringing mercy to his people,
to meet with the man who has mastery of this mount,
seek a truce with the tyrant in return for treasures,
for the time being, until times are better.'

  'You waste your words,' the woman said.
'He cares precious little for land or people,
and reckons nothing to riches and red gold,
but will live as he likes, a law unto himself,
without license or election, his very own lord.
He is mantled in a gown which was made to measure,
spun by specialist Spanish maids,
then gathered together most gracefully in Greece.
It is covered all over in hair, every inch of it,
and bordered with the beards of brilliant kings,
unknotted and combed, so any knight would know
each king by his colour and which country he came from.
Here he rakes in revenues from fifteen realms,
for on the eve of Easter, whenever it falls,
they pay it promptly, for the peace of their people,
have their least-afraid knights deliver it without delay.
For seven winters he awaits answer from Arthur

The old woman's warning

and will stalk this place, plaguing his people
till the King of the British crops off his beard
and it is borne by the bravest of his men to that beast.
If you bring no such beard then it's best you turn tail;
any other offer will end in agony,
for the tally of treasure he takes as he pleases
is higher than any held by Arthur or his elders.
But if you have brought the beard it will bring him more bliss
than a gift of Burgundy or Britain the Greater.
Though in the name of mercy you should mind your mouth,
so no word escapes it, or worse will ensue.
Be prepared with your present, and don't press him too far,
for he sits at his supper and will suddenly see red.
If you heed my advice you will ease from your armour
and kneel in your coat and call him your lord.
This season he savours seven male children,
chopped up on a salver of chalk-white silver
with pickles and powders of precious spices
and plentiful pourings of Portuguese wine.
His spits are spun by three dispirited maidens
who obey his bidding to avoid his bed,
for their lives would be lost in less than four hours
if the filthy urges of his flesh were fulfilled.'

   'I have brought the beard,' he said, 'as is better for me,
and am ready to rush there with it right now,
but first, my dear, inform me where I'll find him,
and if I live I shall laud you, so our Lord help me.'

   'Where the flames of the fire are flaring,' she said,

The woman explains the gift of the beard

'there he feeds his face, to seek as you fancy.
But steal towards him, going sideways from the south,
for he can smell your scent from six miles off.'
Screened by the smoke Arthur sped to the spot,
made the sign of the cross and solemnly swore,
then sidled forward till the fellow was in sight.
How disgusting he was, guzzling and gorging,
lying there lengthways, loathsome and unlordly,
with the haunch of a human thigh in his hand.
His back and his buttocks and his broad limbs
he toasted by the blaze, and his backside was bare.
Appalling and repellent pieces of flesh
of beasts and our brothers were braising there together,
and a cook-pot was crammed with christened children,
some spiked on a spit being spun by maidens.
That noble Sovereign, for the sake of his subjects
his heart bled with hurt on the ground where he halted.
Then he lifted up his shield and delayed no longer,
brandished his broad sword by its bright hilt,
strode straight towards him with a steely spirit
and hailed that hulk with heady words:
'Now may Almighty God, who all men worship,
bring you sorrow and suffering, sot, there where you slouch,
as the foulest figure that was ever formed.
So offensive is your food, may the Fiend have your soul.
On my oath, you oaf, this is odious eating,
these carvings of all creatures. You accursed wretch:
because you have killed these christened children,
making them martyrs, and removed from life
who are cooked on your coals, made corpses at your hands,

Arthur confronts the monster

I shall see you are assigned the vengeance you deserve
through the might of Saint Michael who is master of this
   mount,
and for the fair lady who lies here lifeless
whom you forcibly defiled for your foul pleasure.
So steel yourself, dog's son, may the Devil take your soul,
for you shall die this day by dint of my hands.'

   The startled glutton glared gruesomely,
grinned like a greyhound with grisly fangs,
then groaned and glowered with a menacing grimace,
growling at the good King who greeted him angrily.
His mane and his fringe were filthily matted
and his face was framed in half a foot of foam.
His face and forehead were flecked all over
like the features of a frog, so freckled he seemed.
He was hook-beaked like a hawk, with a hoary beard,
and his eyes were overhung with hairy brows.
To whomever looked hard, as harsh as a hound-fish
was the hide of that hulk, from head to heel.
His ears were huge and a hideous sight,
his eyes were horrid, abhorrent and aflame,
his smile was all sneer, like a flat-mouthed flounder,
and like a bear his fore-teeth were fouled with rank flesh,
and his black, bushy beard grew down to his breast.
He was bulky as a sea-pig with a brawny body,
and each quivering lump of those loathsome lips
writhed and rolled with the wrath of a wolf's head.
He was broad across the back, with the neck of a bull,
badger-breasted with the bristles of a boar,

41   *The monster's hideous appearance*

had arms like oak boughs, wrinkled by age,
and the ugliest loins and limbs, believe me.
He shuffled on his shanks, being shovel-footed,
and his knock-kneed legs were abnormally knuckled.
He was thick in the thigh and like an ogre at the hips,
and as gross as a grease-fed pig – a gruesome sight.
He who mindfully measured that monster's dimension
from face to foot would have found it five fathoms.

    Then he started up sturdily on two strong legs
and quickly copped hold of a club of pure iron
and would have killed the King cleanly with his keen weapon
but by Christ's intervention the vile creature failed,
though Arthur's crest and coronet and silver clasps
went crashing from his helmet with one clatter of that club.
The King then cast up his shield to give cover,
and with his stately sword he stretched out and struck,
fetched him a blow of such force in the forehead
that the burnished blade bit through to his brain.
But he wiped the wound with his foul fingers
and in a flash threw a fist at the other's face;
had the King not been swift in stepping aside
that hit would have ended in a victory for evil.
Then the King countered, followed up fiercely,
caught him high on the hip with his hard weapon,
sinking his sword half a foot through the skin
so the hulk's blood poured hot across the hilt;
through the bladder and bowels he drove that blow,
piercing his privates, ripping them apart.

Arthur wounds the monster

Then he raged and roared, and with a rabid fury
he aimed for Arthur but instead hit the earth,
sundering the soil by the length of a sword,
so the Sovereign almost swooned at the swish of the club.
Yet the King worked quickly, countering cannily,
swiping with his sword so it slashed through the stomach
and the guts and gore came gushing out together
till the grass on the ground was gloupy with slime.
He cast away his club and caught hold of the King,
clinched him in a bear-hug on the crest of the crag,
clamped him ever closer, crushing his ribs,
holding him so hard his heart almost burst.
Then those melancholy maidens fell to the floor,
kneeling and praying and pleading for this knight:
'Let Christ bring him comfort and keep him from sorrow,
and defend him from the fiend who would finish his life.'

But the muscles of the warlock overwhelmed the monarch,
and they writhed and wrestled riotously together,
weltering and wallowing through the wild bushes,
tumbling and toppling and tearing at clothes,
rolling from the ridge in an unruly muddle
with Arthur now over, then under, then over,
from the height of the hill to where hard rocks were heaped,
not slacking though they slugged it out along the shore.
Then Arthur did damage with the dagger he had drawn,
hammering that hulk right up to the hilt,
but he throttled him so thoroughly in the throws of death
that he broke three rib-bones in the royal man's breast.

43   *Arthur delivers the fatal blow*

Then keen Sir Kay came quickly and cried:
'Alas, we are lost, my lord is done for,
confounded by a fiend, our fate is sealed:
we are finished and forced into flight forever.'
They heaved off Arthur's hauberk and with their hands
    examined him,
from the haunches of his hips to the heights of his shoulders,
then his flanks and loins and his fine limbs,
then his back and breast and his bare arms,
and were jubilant when they found that his flesh remained
    flawless,
gentle knights, made joyful by such justice.
'For certain,' said Sir Bedivere, 'it seems, by my Saviour,
he seeks fewer saints the more strongly he seizes them,
he who carts such a corpse from above the cliff-tops
and carries the creature to encase him in silver.
By Michael, at such a man I am forced to marvel,
that our Lord should allow him to enter heaven,
for if all saints who serve our Lord are the same
then by my father's soul I shall never be a saint!'
The wise King replied wittily to Bedivere's words:
'I have sought out this saint, so help me my Saviour;
now unsheathe your sword and skewer his heart,
and make certain of this, soldier, for he has sorely grieved me.
I have not fought such a fellow in fifteen winters,
though in the Aran Mountains I once met such a man
more fearless and forceful than any fighter by far,
who would have felled me that day had fortune been
    unfavourable.
Now hack off his head and impale it on a pike,

        Arthur's knights find their King alive

hand it to your squire with his steadfast steed,
then bear it to Sir Howell who is broken-hearted,
and bid him to think better, now his enemy lies butchered.
Then hurry it to Barfleur and house it in iron,
and mount it on the main-gate for all men to see.
My sword and strong shield are still strewn on the earth
at the crest of that crag where we first clashed,
and close by, the club which is cast in iron
that has killed so many Christians in the lands of Cotentin.
Trek to the top and retrieve the weapon,
then we go forward to our fleet which floats on the tide.
Any treasure which tempts you, you are welcome to take,
I have the coat and the club, and covet nothing more.'

So they climbed to the crag, those noble knights,
brought back the broad shield and shining sword,
Sir Kay carrying the coat and the club,
then accompanied the Conqueror to explain to the kings
what in secret their Sovereign had kept to himself,
while the blue sky brightened above clearing clouds.

Now a clamouring group had gathered at court,
who knelt as one before the noble King.
'Welcome, our liege lord, too long you were away.
Governor under God, great in your actions,
to whom grace is granted and given at His will,
now your presence in this place brings comfort and peace.
Through your royal right your people have revenge!
By your helping hand our enemy is destroyed,
who overran your lords and robbed them of their little ones.

Arthur is praised for his bravery

No realm in disarray was so readily relieved!'
Then the Conqueror replied with Christian courtesy:
'Thank God for this grace, which He alone granted;
for it was no man's deed, but the doing of our Deity,
or a miracle of His Mother who gives mercy to all.'

Then speedily he summoned those shipmen in his service
to look sharp with his shire-men and share out the goods.
'Take all the treasure stolen by that traitor
to commoners in the countryside, to clergy and others;
your duty is to deal it amongst my dear subjects,
so no person, at your peril, complains of his portion.'
With kingly words he commanded his cousin
to found a church on the crag where the corpse still lay,
with a convent inside where Christ could be served,
in memory of the Duchess who was martyred on the mount.

Now that Arthur the King had killed the ogre,
he went briskly in bright mood from Barfleur next morning
with his battalion about him by those beautiful brooks;
towards Castle Blank he chose the best course,
through a pretty, open plain, under chalky hills;
at each fresh torrent he found a place to ford
and with his kindly company crossed as he liked.
Then that stern Sovereign set up his tents,
formed a stronghold by a stream on a stretch of land.

Shortly after midday, when mealtime was done,
there arrived two messengers of those remote marches,
from the Marshal of France, who met him with good manners,

The British make camp in France

seeking his assistance and saying these words:
'Sir, your marshal and minister, through your powerful majesty,
beseeches that your mercy might save your subjects,
those men of the marches who are mired in mayhem
and suffer great strife despite strenuous defence.
Now hear that the Emperor has entered into France
with hosts of our enemies, horrible and huge.
In Burgoyne he burns your cities like bonfires
and butchers your barons who live in its buildings;
with a vast force of arms violently he invades
the countries and castles which belong to your crown,
cutting down your commoners, clergy and others;
without your care, my King, they will never recover.
He fells many forests and forays through your lands,
affords no pardons and brings fear to each fellow,
slaying your subjects and seizing their possessions.
To the fair tongue of France these foreigners are fatal.
He tears through tender territories, so the German folk tell,
under banners draped with dreaded dragons,
sending to the slaughter by the slash of swords
all those dukes and peers who dwell in that place.
So the lords of the land and their ladies beg you,
for the love of Peter, the apostle of Rome,
since you camp in this country, to engage in combat
with that terrorizing tyrant, before time runs out.
He inhabits those hills beneath the high forest
with a huge host of heathen knights.
Help us, for His love, who resides in highest heaven,
and speak boldly to those who bring us to oblivion.'

Arthur hears of the Roman invasion

The King bade bold Sir Boice, 'Go, briskly!
Take Sir Berill with you and Sir Bedivere the brave,
and Sir Gawain and Sir Gerin, both gallant knights,
go at a gallop to those far green woods,
giving word to Sir Lucius that his ways are unworthy,
flouting the law most foully with my folk.
I shall stop him where he stands, if I stay alive,
or many who follow him will be found fallen.
Instruct him sternly, in no uncertain terms,
to retreat from my kingdom with his notorious troops.
And in case that cursed wretch should decline,
have him come, out of courtesy, for single combat,
and we shall soon reassess the right he asserts
to make riot in this realm and ravage the people.
Dreaded blows shall deal out death,
the Lord at Doomsday shall do as he likes!'

They made ready for the ride, those noble knights,
glittering with gold upon their great steeds,
and went towards the woods with whetted weapons
to greet the grand lord who was soon to find grief.

Then those honoured ones halted at the edge of a holt,
and beheld the fine housings of the heathen kings,
and heard coming from the camp a chorus of hundreds,
with herds of elephants trumpeting from their trunks.
Rich tents were erected, their walls arrayed
with silk and purple and precious stones.
Pennants and pommels of princes' coats of arms
were pitched in the valley for people to view.

48   *British knights visit the Roman encampment*

The Romans themselves had arranged their rich tents
in a row by the river beneath the round hills,
with the Emperor's, with due honour, exactly at the heart,
emblazoned all over with bold-looking eagles.
And they spied him, with the Sultan and many senators,
processing through the site with sixteen kings
who glided serenely together as a group
to dine with their sovereign on dishes of delicacies.

Then they went over water, those worshipful knights,
and rode through woods to where the regal Romans
were washed and at table. Going at once towards them,
worthy Gawain spoke these withering words:
'May the might and majesty that honours us all,
who are formed and fashioned by His force alone,
bring sorrow to your seats, Sultan and everyone
who meet in this hall. May you men be miserable!
And the empty heretic who calls himself Emperor,
who rules without right the Empire of Rome,
Sir Arthur's heritage, that honourable King,
which was owned by all of his ancestors but Uther,
may the curse that Cain incurred through his brother
cling to you, cuckoo, loafing there in your crown,
the least of all lords that I ever looked on.
By my word, my master has to wonder why this man
goes slaying his subjects who deserve no such grief,
common country folk, clergy and others,
who are wholly innocent and ignorant in warfare.
So the notable King, courteous and noble,
urgently orders you out of his lands,

Sir Gawain addresses Lucius

or come at once and encounter him in combat.
Let your coveting of the crown be declared to all.
My duty here is finished, defy me if you dare
before all your followers, chieftains and all fellows.
State for us your response and stall no further,
that we may leave without loitering and deliver it to my lord.'

    The Emperor responded, speaking most sternly:
'You are sent from my enemy, Sir Arthur himself,
and to injure his knights would bring harm to my honour,
though you are angry men who run his errands.
Were it not out of reverence to my right royal table
you would rue at once the rudeness of your words.
That such lowly stock should insult these lords,
so nobly and royally arrayed with their retinue!
But speak to your sovereign, for I send him these words:
I will linger hereabouts for as long as I like,
then for solace will saunter along Seine
besieging every city by the salt strands,
then ride by the Rhone which runs so sweetly
and crash down the walls of his worthy castles.
In Paris, as time passes, as proof of my point,
I shall leave him not half of a levelled haycock.'

    'Now certainly,' said Sir Gawain, 'well might I wonder,
that a simpleton like yourself should dare such a speech.
Rather than own the realm of fair France
I'd faithfully fight with you face to face.'

    Then Sir Gayous answered with high-toned arrogance,

Gawain and Lucius trade insults

being uncle to the Emperor and himself an earl:
'These Britons were always blusterers and braggarts.
Lo, how he swaggers in his shining suit
as if to brutalise us all with the bright sword he brandishes.
But his bark is all boast, that boy who stands there.'

Then Gawain, being wounded by those wild words,
flew at that fellow with fire in his heart;
with his steely sword he struck off his head,
then leapt to his steed and sped away with his lords.
Through the guardsmen they galloped, the gallant knights,
stampeding past soldiers who stood in their path;
over water they went, hurtling on horseback,
only breaking for breath at the wood's border.
Countless foe came after, following on foot,
and Romans on their royally arrayed mounts,
pursuing our proud men through the open plain
on chalk-white horses to a high, wooded chase.
And one fellow in fine gold finished with sable
rode foremost on his Frisian in flaming armour,
flourishing a weapon, fabulously fashioned,
coming fast on our folk with a fierce war-cry.

Then good Sir Gawain on his grey steed
gripped a great spear and speedily spiked him;
through the guts and gore his weapon glided
till the sharpened steel sliced into his heart.
The man and his horse lay heaped on the earth,
and he groaned in grief at his grisly wounds.
Then a proudly arrayed rider pressed upon them,

Gawain decapitates the uncle of Lucius

sporting on his shield the silver-striped purple,
bounding boldly into battle on his brown steed –
he was a pagan of Persia, this person in pursuit.
Sir Boice, unflustered, met this foe with force,
ran through him thoroughly with a thrust of his lance,
so both soldier and broad shield lay shattered on the ground,
then he brought out the blade and withdrew to his brothers.

Then Sir Feltemour, a man much merited for his might,
came belting forward with his blood boiling,
going for Sir Gawain, girded into action
out of grief for Sir Gayous who lay dead on the ground.
Sir Gawain was glad; against him he galloped
with Galuth, his great sword, and struck him gravely,
hacking in half the knight on horseback,
cleaving him most cleanly through his body from his crown,
thus slaying the knight with his celebrated sword.

Then a royal man of Rome roared out to his lords:
'We shall rue our fortune if we follow further.
Those are boastful braggarts who brew up such evil,
foul fate befell him that first named them so!'

So the royal Romans, with a twist of the reins,
returned to their tents to tell their company
how Sir Marshall de Mowne was mortally mown down,
out-jousted for his japery in the day's jaunt.
But a cantering cavalry still chased our knights
on their fast steeds, five thousand fellows
in their wake, towards woods, through surging white water

The Romans give chase

that flowed from a lake some fifty miles afar.
There the Britons and baronets abided in ambush;
the chosen chiefs of the King's chamber
watched the foe run amuck among our men and our mounts,
chopping down our chieftains who challenged their eminence.
Then the Britons all at once burst from the ambush,
boldly flying banners, all Bedivere's knights,
they raced at the Romans that rode by the woods,
all those royal ranks that were loyal to Rome,
falling urgently on the enemy and eagerly striking,
all the earls of England, and 'Arthur' they cried.
Through armour and bright shields they breached men's breasts,
the boldest of Britons with their battle-sharpened swords.
There the Romans were routed and roundly wounded,
chastened like churls by chivalrous knights.
In disarray, the ruined Romans retreated,
fell back and fled – out of fear it seems!

Now a spokesman approaches Senator Peter,
saying, 'Sir, it is certain that your forces are defeated.'
At once he assembled an army of ten thousand,
and by the salt strands suddenly set upon our men.
The Britons reeled, and were rattled a little,
but the bold bannerets and the bachelor knights
broke the battle-line with the breasts of their chargers;
Sir Boice and his men dealt out bitter blows.
Then the Romans rearranged their battalions and rallied,
went hacking through our fighters on their fresh horses,
overturning the truest ranks of the Round Table,
riding through the rearguard, wreaking great grief.

The Romans are ambushed by the British

Then the battling Britons held their line no longer,
but quit the field and fled to the forest;
Sir Berill was borne down and Sir Boice seized,
the best of our brave men were bloodily wounded,
yet our soldiers stood at a stronghold for a while,
astounded by the strokes of those stout knights,
and were stricken with sorrow for their captain who was captured,
and sought God to send succour as He saw fit.

Then up rode Sir Idrus, heavily armed,
with five hundred men mounted on fine horses,
urgently asking for news of our army,
and how far away were those friends who had fled.
Then Sir Gawain said, 'By the grace of God,
today we were hunted and driven like hares,
overrun by Romans on their royal steeds
as we quaked under cover like cowardly wretches.
May I never look upon my lord in my life
if we serve him so woefully, whom we once pleased so well.'

Then the stout-hearted Britons spurred on their steeds
and fearlessly went flying back into the fray,
the fierce men at the front roaring ferociously,
riding through the forest with refreshed fervour.
The Romans had better arrayed their ranks
in one wide row, and readied their weapons;
their legions were ranged in a line along the river
with Sir Boice in the grip of aggressive guards.
Now along the salt strands they unleashed their assault,
stalwarts striking their stern blows,

Sir Boice is captured

colliding with impressive lances held aloft,
in lordly livery on their leaping horses,
skewering our soldiers on sharpened spikes
so they gasped and gaped with ghastly expressions.
Great lords of Greece who were gored and maimed
still summoned up the strength to exchange swift strokes,
and dying knights were dealt their death-blow.
So many that were struck just stumbled in a stupor,
and all met their maker on the field where they fell.
Gallant Sir Gawain made gains through huge efforts,
greeting their greatest with grievous wounds;
with Galuth he knocked down the most notable knights,
striking grimly for grief of the lord so great.
Regally he rode, then charged in rapidly
to where bold Sir Boice was held in bounds,
hacking through armour and hauberks and helmets,
liberating that lord and leading him to safety.
Senator Peter pursued him at speed
through the thick of the throng with his royal riders,
openly proving his prowess to that prisoner,
flanked by a host of expert horsemen.
Dishonourably from behind he hacked at Sir Gawain,
fetched him a brutal blow with his blade,
ripping his hauberk in half at the rear,
yet Sir Boice was brought clear of those black-hearted brawlers.

Then boldly the Britons blared their bugles
and, elated that Sir Boice was broken from his bonds,
they weighed back into battle, bringing down knights,
rupturing breastplates with burnished blades,

Gawain frees Sir Boice

striking steeds with steel swords at the height of the struggle
and scything down strongly all who stood in their sight.
Sir Idrus Fitz Ewain then shouted out, 'Arthur!'
and assailed the senator with sixteen knights
of the sturdiest stock that belonged to our side,
assaulting them as one with that small squadron,
falling fiercely on the vanguard with flaming swords,
then fighting the front-line with refreshed fortitude,
until many of those foreign forces lay felled
on the fair field by those fresh streams.

Then Sir Idrus Fitz Ewain swung into action,
launched in alone with lusty lashes,
sought out the senator and seized his reins,
and delivered a warning of wisely chosen words:
'Yield, sir, if you yearn to see more years,
though what presents you proffer will not promise a pardon;
truly, if you stall or try any of your tricks
you shall die by dint of my hands this day.'

'I surrender,' said the senator, 'so help me my Saviour,
but only on condition of an audience with King Arthur,
and treat me with reason, for readily I can raise
such revenue from Rome as my ransom requires.'

Then Sir Idrus answered with hard words:
'The King shall decide the conditions of your capture
when you come to be tried by the court and his kinsmen;
he may counsel to keep you alive no longer
and command you be killed before his company of knights.'

Senator Peter surrenders

They marched him through the men and hauled off his
   armour
and left him to Lionel and Lowell his brother.
So along those lowlands, by the lovely waters,
many lords of Sir Lucius were lost forever:
Senator Peter was secured as a prisoner,
and peerless knights of Persia and Port Jaffa
and plenty beside had perished in that place.
In the mayhem at the ford some fell to the flood;
there the Romans could be witnessed with their rueful wounds,
overrun by the ranks of the Round Table,
and they straightened their hauberks at the side of the stream
which ran already with ruby red blood.
The unruly prisoners were placed at the rearguard
to ransom for red gold and royal steeds.
Hurriedly they all hopped onto fresh horses,
and on a route to the King they rode right away.

A horseman went ahead to speak with King Arthur:
'Sir, your messengers come merrily out of the mountains;
we were met today by men of the marches
and mutilated in the melee by marvellous knights.
Faithfully we fought by those far, fresh streams,
with the fiercest fighters belonging to your foe.
Fifty thousand on the field, fearsome battlers,
are all fallen to their fate in a single furlong.
Our Lord alone allowed us our lives.
Of those fine forces who assailed your fellows
the Chancellor of Rome, a royal chief,
will plead for charity and a charter of peace.

Arthur is informed of the battle

Senator Peter is seized as a prisoner;
scores of pagans from Persia and Port Jaffa
are now steered on their steeds by your stout knights
to a penance of pain and poverty in your jails.
I beseech you, sir, to speak your wish:
would you have them released or delivered to our Lord?
Some sixty steeds you might receive for the senator,
all saddled with silver and sent here by Saturday,
and in exchange for that chevalier the noble Chief Chancellor
chariots charged with chests full of gold.
What remnants of the Romans still remain shall be held
till their revenues from Rome are rightly reckoned.
Sir, I beseech you, let these lords be certain
if you send them overseas or insist they remain.
All your highest lords still have their health
bar Sir Ewain Fitz Henry who is injured to his side.'

    'Thank Christ and his cherished mother,' exclaimed Arthur,
'that by His acts you were helped and heartened.
By wise ways God works His wonders,
no wretch or rogue or can outrun His reach.
Where fate and fortune in fighting are concerned
all is deemed and dealt out by the will of our Deity.
I am grateful for your coming, it comforts our gathering.
Sir knight,' said the Conqueror, 'so Christ help me,
for these tidings I treat you to the treasure that is Toulouse,
its toll and its takings, its taverns and all else,
the town and its tenements with their high towers,
and all belonging to the laity, for as long as I shall live.
But warn the senator to witness these words:

Arthur welcomes the news of victory

no silver will save him unless Ewain survives.
I would sooner him sink in the sand by the salt-streams
than my worthy knight be unwell with his wounds.
His brigades I shall break up, so Christ help me,
and send them in solitude to the lands of other sovereigns.
He shall look on his lords in Rome no longer,
nor sit in the assembly in sight of the senate;
it is unbecoming for a King who is Conqueror
to settle with insurgents through desire for silver.
As he knows full well, it is never for a knight
to bargain and do business with bound captives,
and improper for a prisoner to press his captor
or appear in his presence while business is practised.
Order the constable who keeps the castle
to secure the convict in close confinement.
Before midday tomorrow he shall hear the command
of what land he will live in, like it or not.'

So the captive was conveyed by armed company
to the custody of the constable as the King had instructed,
and returning to Arthur they were eager to tell
how the Emperor answered and his angry reaction.
Then Arthur, noblest above anyone on earth,
at the meal in the evening was admiring of his men.
'These I honour beyond anything under heaven,
who in my absence were so heroic in their actions;
I shall love them while I live, so help me Lord,
and allow them all the ample acres they have earned.
All my life's length this game they shall not lose
who were lamed out of loyalty by these lovely waters.'

59   *Arthur declines to ransom the prisoners*

But by day's dawning the dearest of kings
called on Sir Cador with his noble comrades,
Sir Cleremus, Sir Cleremond and fellow combatants
Sir Clowdmur and Sir Clegis, to escort the captives;
and Sir Boice and Sir Berill with their banners displayed,
and Sir Baldwin, Sir Brian, brave Sir Bedivere,
Sir Raynald and Sir Richard, the sons of Sir Rowland,
to ride with the Romans, escorting their ranks.
'Speed stealthily by steed to splendid Paris,
with the prisoner Peter and his knightly peers,
and place them with the provost in the presence of lords,
and make it plain that on pain of peril
they be watched closely and kept in their quarters
by wise wardens and worthy knights.
Let him spare no silver in hiring such sentries;
he is well warned, beware if he fails.'
Then the Britons moved busily at the bidding of their King,
embarked in their battle-gear with banners displayed;
they chased towards Chartres, those chivalrous knights,
peerless and proud through the province of Champagne.

But meanwhile the mighty Emperor had ordered
two honourable knights, Sir Utolf and Sir Evander,
both earls of the Orient, with their hardened knights,
and the wiliest warriors in the whole of his host,
Sir Sextynour of Libya and several senators,
the King of Syria with swarms of Saracens,
and the Senator of Sutri with a sizable army,
being assigned on that sortie by assent of his peers,
to trek towards Troyes with treachery in mind,

The prisoners are escorted towards Paris

to trick and to trap our travelling knights,
having heard that Peter would be housed in Paris,
imprisoned by the provost to pay his penance.
They made ready and rode with their banners raised,
headed through woodland on huge horses,
took position on the path, powerfully placed
to prise back the prisoners from our peerless knights.

Then Sir Cador of Cornwall commanded his comrades,
Sir Clegis, Sir Cleremus, Sir Cleremond the noble:
'Here's the Cutting of Clime with its lofty cliffs;
check the passage is clear, for there is plentiful cover;
make a sweeping search of the shrubs and bushes
for any scoundrel who skulks there and might scoff at us later.
Be diligent in this duty or we ride into danger,
and such a furtive foe can never be defeated.'
So they galloped to the woods, those gallant warriors,
in loyalty to their lords, to listen for the enemy,
and discovered them armed and armoured on their horses
waiting on the wayside at the hem of the woods.
With courtly countenance Sir Clegis himself
cried to the company with these clear words:
'Will any noble knight or kaiser of note
prove his love for his leader through his craft in combat?
We have come from the King of this fair country,
who across the whole earth is crowned the Conqueror,
the royal retinues of the Round Table
who are willing at his word to ride and rout.
Should any be forthcoming, we request armed contest
with notable knights who are loyal to their lords.

Roman knights intercept the prisoner convoy

Is their anyone here, be it earl or otherwise,
who will venture into action on behalf of his Emperor?'

    An angry earl answered him eagerly:
'I am furious with Arthur and his famous followers,
who thus in error occupies this area
and outrages the Emperor, his earthly ruler.
The reputation of the royal Round Table
is recounted with rancour across regions and realms
for revelling without right in the revenues of Rome.
If justice is ours he'll be held to answer,
and plenty who ride in his ranks shall repent
for the crude conduct of their reckless King.'

    'Ah,' said Sir Clegis, 'So help me Christ,
it appears from your parlance you're a penny-pincher;
but be you auditor, earl or the Emperor himself,
I answer at once on Arthur's behalf.
The royal King who rightfully rules us,
the true and trusted knights of the Round Table,
he has read through the rolls and prepared the records,
and will execute a reckoning you shall rue for ever,
that all Rome's powerful people shall repent
before rents and revenues are rightfully repaid.
By your courtesy we crave three contests of joust,
where the victor shall earn both horse and arms.
You trick us today with your trifling words,
treachery typical of itinerant travellers.
So send out your sternest knights this second
or say with sincerity that you would sooner surrender!'

                                              Sir Clegis challenges the Romans

Then the King of Syria said, 'So save me Christ;
delay all day long, no duel shall be delivered
till you pledge a promise to my proud knights
that your coat and crest are accredited by lords
as arms of ancestry with ownership of lands.'

'Sir King,' said Sir Clegis, 'How grandly you counter.
But I wonder if those words are the work of a coward.
The ancestry of my arms is acknowledged by the highest;
my banner has borne them since the time of Brutus,
and at the time when the city of Troy was besieged
was often seen with our knights on assault.
Then Brutus brought us with our bold forebears
aboard his boats to Britain the Greater.'

'Sir,' said Sir Sextynour, 'say what you please,
and we shall suffer your speeches as is deemed seemly.
Then truss up your trumpets and trifle no longer;
dally all the day but you are destined to fail,
for never shall a Roman who rides in my ranks
be rebuked by a boor while I abide on this earth.'

Then Sir Clegis inclined with a bow to that king
and returned to Sir Cador with these courteous tidings:
'We have found in that forest where the leaves flourish
a flowering of folk who belong to your foe,
a force of fifty thousand of the fiercest armed fighters,
all primed for battle under those brimming boughs,
in ambush on horseback with their banners in the air,
in the wood of beeches that borders the way.

Clegis reports to Sir Cador

They defend the ford where the water runs fairest,
so our only way forward is to face them with force.
So it follows that today our fate will be told,
be it fight or flight, fall as it may.'
'Never,' Sir Cador cried, 'so help me Christ;
to shun or shirk from so little would be shameful.
Sir Lancelot, who lodges with the King, shall not laugh
that my path was hindered by anyone on this earth;
I would die and be undone before dallying this day
out of dread of some dog's son in those dim bushes.'

    Sir Cador then courteously comforted his comrades,
called to them with keen and courageous words:
'Envisage our valiant prince, who provides us
with lands and lordships to suit our liking,
who has dealt to us dukedoms and dubbed us knights,
who has given us gold and granted many gifts,
greyhounds, great horses and endless games
to delight any lord who lives under God.
Never shall the royal reputation of the Round Table
be wrenched from us and ripped by Romans on this earth.
Do not spar sparsely or spare any weapons
but fight ferociously like fearless warriors.
I would be boiled alive and butchered into quarters
before failing my duty while so full of fury.'

    Then that indomitable duke dubbed his knights,
Ioneke and Askanere, Aladuke and others
that were heirs of Essex and those eastern marches,
Howell and Hardolf who were fortunate in arms,

Cador issues a war cry

Sir Heryll and Sir Herygall, two hard-headed knights.
Then he singled out certain knights for assignment,
Sir Baldwin, Sir Uriel and Sir Bedivere the brave,
and Raynald and Richard, children of Rowland:
'Protect our Prince with your peerless knights,
and if by our bravery we fare best in battle
then stay in this place and stray not one stride.
But if chance should choose that we are beaten in the charge,
then escape to some castle and save your souls,
or gallop to the King if the coast is clear
and have him ride in a rush to rescue his men.'

Then the steely Britons shouldered their shields,
pulled helmets to their heads and held their lances high;
thus he arranged his ranks and rode to the field
with a force of five hundred with lances aimed forwards.
To trumpets they travelled, on horses in their trappings,
to cornets and clarions and clear, clever notes,
stalling no longer but storming in suddenly
to where shrubs shone under shimmering trees.
Then the Roman troops retreated a little,
and our royal rearguard rushed to the breach,
so rapidly that they rang with the sound of rivets
and burnished metal and bright chain-mail.

Then the enemy shot out from under shelter of shrubbery
all at once, wielding great weapons of war.
The King of Libya with his loyal liegemen
advanced the vanguard, voicing the battle-cry;
then this cruel leader levelled his lance

The British charge into battle

and held on a course towards an armoured horse,
bearing down on Sir Berill, and brutally struck,
grievously gouging him through the gullet and the neck-piece.
The man and his mount lay sprawled in the mud;
he spoke softly to his Saviour and surrendered his soul.
So brave Sir Berill was broken and lifeless
and lay there for the burial that bold men deserve.

  Then Sir Cador of Cornwall was saddened to the core
that his loyal comrade was laid low.
He embraced the body and kissed Sir Berill,
commanded his good men to gather and guard him.
And the Libyan King was heard laughing loudly:
'I like it better now that lord has leapt off!
He won't bother us today, the devil have his bones.'

  'That King,' said Sir Cador, 'is careless with his tongue;
since he killed this kinsman – Christ keep your soul –
he shall count the cost, if Christ will help me.
We shall duel to the death before this day is done;
sure as wind turns the windmill, so I'll have my way,
finishing him forever, or felling his friends.'
Then courageous Sir Cador drove keenly into battle,
cried 'For Cornwall!' launching in with a levelled lance;
he struck straight through the throng on his sturdy steed,
stopping many a stout man with his singular strength.
When his spear splintered he sped on eagerly,
unsheathed his sword that served well with each swipe,
slashing wide swathes and scything down men,
leaving wounded warriors writhing in his wake;

Sir Berill is killed by the King of Libya

he hacked at the hardiest and hewed them at the neck,
and all ran with red wherever he rode,
so that many bold lords said goodbye to their lives.
He tilted at tyrants and tore them from their saddles,
then turned from the turmoil when the time seemed best.

Then the Libyan King called out loudly
to intrepid Sir Cador with taunting talk:
'By winning yourself worship and wounding many knights
you warrant that you own the whole of the world.
But on my word, I wait and welcome your attack,
so beware if you will, I have warned you well.'

Then as clarions called, the newly named knights
responded to the sound by raising their spears;
they headed the front rank on iron-hued horses,
and fifty of their foe were felled in one charge.
They shot through the shields, shattering shafts,
and honourable lords were left in a heap
as our newly dubbed knights used their strength nobly.
But some dirty new deed annoys me deeply:
that Libyan had stolen a steed that suited him,
and with a shield of silver lions launched in all lord-like,
surrounding the ranks and causing a rift,
and by his lance many men to their maker were sent.
Thus he chased and assaulted our Sovereign's chosen subjects,
killing knights on campaign across the countryside,
and unsparingly with his hunting spear he spiked many.

Sir Aladuke was slain and Sir Achinour injured,

The King of Libya's killing spree

and Sir Origge and Sir Ermyngall hacked to pieces;
then they latched hold of Lewlin and Lewlin's brother
and lords of Libya led them to their stronghold.
Had Sir Clegis and Clement the noble not been near
young men and many more would have met their doom.

Then courageous Sir Cador readied his spear,
a cruel looking lance, and launched at the king,
hit him heavily on the helmet with a hard blow
so his hands were bathed in his enemy's hot blood.
Now the evil heathen king lay heaped on the earth
and was so mortally maimed he would never mend.
Then keen Sir Cador called out loudly:
'You are served what you sowed, may our Saviour bring you
      sorrow
for the killing of my comrade. Now my cares are lightened.
Find comfort if you can as you cool in the clay.
You baited us many times with your brash boasts;
this misfortune you find is of your own manufacture.
Keep hold of what you have, it will harm no other,
for hatred comes home to the hand that chose it.'

The King of Syria was then stricken with sorrow
for the sake of that sovereign who was set upon and slain;
he assembled a party of Saracens and senators
and viciously they advanced on our various men.
But Sir Cador of Cornwall countered them at once
with his mightiest men in fighting formation;
where the path went forward in front of the forest
fifty thousand folk were quickly felled,

Cador kills the King of Libya

and in battle the boldest knights on both sides
were horribly injured at the height of the action.
The fiercest Saracens who fought with their forces
shot six feet out of their saddles when struck;
those knights who sheltered behind shields were shattered,
men in their mail were mortally wounded;
through burnished plate many breasts were pierced.
Armguards burst open, horses were hacked,
and blood-smeared shields smashed to smithereens
from high-striding steeds with shining steel swords.
The Britons manfully maimed so many
the broad field they battled on was a running blood-bath.
By now Sir Cador had captured a captain,
and Sir Clegis quickly caught another in his clutches,
The Captain of Corneto, who besides the king
held the key to the countryside all along that coast.
Utolf and Evander were held by Ioneke
with the Earl of Africa and other great lords.
The King of Syria had surrendered to Sir Cador
and the Seneschal of Sutri had submitted to Sagramour.
When the chevaliers saw their chieftains shackled in chains
they chose to flee to a fecund forest,
and they felt so faint they fell in the groves
among ferns of the woods in fear of our folk.
Our royal troops were seen riding through trees,
rooting out and ripping up the wounded Romans,
hollering after heathens and heinous knights,
and they hacked down hundreds at the border of the bushes.
So our chivalrous men gave chase to those charlatans,
and the few that broke clear escaped to a castle.

69   *The British win a bloody battle*

Then the ranks of the Round Table regrouped and rallied,
and hurtled through the holt where the Duke had halted,
searching the brushwood and bringing back those brothers
who had fallen to their fates in the day's fighting.
Sir Cador had them covered in fine cloths
and carried by cart to the King by good knights,
then proceeded to Paris with the prisoners himself
and passed them to the provost, princes and everyone,
and dined in the tower but did not dally,
going quickly to the King to recount what had happened:
'Sir,' said Sir Cador, 'an encounter occurred.
We clashed today all across the countryside
with kings and kaisers both unkind and honoured,
and with knights and nobles copiously equipped.
At the woods they stood like a wall in our way,
and at the ford in the forest their forces were armed.
There we fought and fenced with those men in good faith,
on the field with your army, and felled many foe.
The King of Libya is laid low,
and loyal liegemen who belonged to that lord.
Combatants from other countries are also captured
and are delivered here to live or die as you like.
Sir Utolf and Sir Evander, both honourable knights,
were seized by Ioneke by a heroic feat of arms,
along with earls of the Orient and other hardened leaders
whose allegiance and bloodlines are loyal to that host.
The Senator Barouns has been bound by our brigade,
and the Captain of Corneto, renowned for his cruel streak,
along with the unsavoury Seneschal of Sutri
and the King of Syria himself with his Saracens.

Cador reports the victory to Arthur

But fourteen of our knights lie fallen in the field,
I will not hide the facts, but inform you of them faithfully:
Sir Berill is one, a brave banneret,
who was killed in the first clash by a royal king,
and Sir Aladuke of Towell with his trustworthy troops
was taken by the Turks and in time found dead.
And Sir Mawrelle of Maunces and his brother Mawrene,
and Sir Meneduke of Mentoch with his marvellous men.'

Then the worthy King wept, his eyes full of woe,
and spoke to his cousin Sir Cador these words:
'Sir Cador, your courage will be the ruin of this Court.
The cream of my knights are cast down through your cowardice:
to imperil men by impetuousness is no prize worth possessing,
unless the parties were prepared and empowered for war.
You should have stood firm in the safety of the stronghold,
for in straying you destroy my stalwarts in one stroke.'

'Sir,' said Sir Cador, 'as King of this country
you may speak as you want, as you are well aware.
But no knight who boards here shall ever rebuke me
that his boasting barred me from doing your bidding.
When any company goes campaigning, grant them copious
    equipment,
or in those cruel lands they will be confounded and crushed.
Today I did my duty – let lords judge my diligence –
and in danger of death I faced dreaded knights.
Yet you grant me no grace, just your great words,
and in speaking what I feel my fortune is no fairer.'

Cador's actions have displeased Arthur

And though Sir Arthur was angered he answered justly:
'You have acted doughtily, Sir Duke, in arms,
and have done your duty with my undaunted knights;
and without doubt you are deemed by dukes and earls
one of the noblest knights that was ever known.
On this earth no offspring have I issued at all:
you are the heir apparent, or a child of your own;
you are my sister's son, so I shall never forsake you.'

Then he ordered attendants to set a table in his tent,
and with trumpets he welcomed his weary warriors,
served them solemnly with succulent food
upon silver salvers, a most special sight.

When the senators heard tell of these twists and turns,
they told the Emperor, 'Your troops are taken.
Sir Arthur, your enemy, has ousted your lords
who rode to the rescue of those royal knights.
In taking your time you distress your people;
you are betrayed by men whom you truly trusted.
This will torture and torment you for time without end.'

Then the Emperor was irate, angered to his heart,
that the pride of our people had won such prowess.
With king and with kaiser he called a council,
with Saracen sovereigns and many senators.
So his special lords were soon assembled,
and to the group who were gathered he gave these words:
'My heart is set, with the seal of your assent,
to march into Soissons with my mightiest men,

Defeat is reported to Lucius

and give fight to my foe, if fortune allows it;
in no half of the earth will my enemy hide.
Or to enter Autun in search of an escapade,
and stay in that city with my staunch followers,
to rest and revel and be as riotous as we please,
living life to the full in those fruitful lands,
until Sir Leo and his loyal ranks arrive
with the lords of Lombardy, to prevent his advance.'

But our wise King was wary and watchful of his enemy,
and did well by withdrawing his warriors from the woods;
he fed the fires which flamed at his camp
then stowed all possessions and stole away stealthily.
Without stalling for a second he went straight on to Soissons,
and by the rising of the sun had sectioned his ranks,
quickly cordoning the city on all sides
with seven great checkpoints, bringing access to a halt.
And in a valley set a vanguard to watch for visitors:
Sir Valiant of Wales with his valorous warriors
had vowed in view of the King's visage
to vanquish through victory the Viscount of Rome,
and was chosen by the King, however chance might change,
to be chieftain when the enemy were charged upon and
    checked.
And he delegated duties to his trusted deputies,
but command of the main guard remained with the King.
He set out his foot-soldiers as he found fitting,
and the first-rank was filled with his finest knights.
Then he ordered his archers to both halves thereafter,
to shape as a shield-wall and shoot when ordered.

The British decamp to Soissons

He arrayed in the rearguard his most royal knights,
renowned nobles of the Round Table,
Sir Raynald, Sir Richard who was rarely fearful,
the Duke of Rouen with many dozens of riders;
Sir Kay and Sir Clegis, so the King declared,
should watch with warriors by the clear running waters.
Sir Lot and Sir Lancelot, those lordly knights,
would lie to his left with ranks in reserve
to move in by morning if needs must.
And Sir Cador of Cornwall and his keen knights
would keep watch at the crossroads close by the others;
he placed at such posts many princes and earls
so no person could pass by any secret path.

So afterwards, when the Emperor, with honoured knights
and earls went adventuring into the valley,
he ran into King Arthur whose armies were arrayed,
ready for his arrival, and to add to his anguish
our brave, bold King had entered the battlefield
with battalions in formation and banners unfurled.
He had set up blockades to all sides of the city,
every cliff and gully was guarded by good men;
in the marshes and high mountains and mossy swamps
mobs of great fighters would meet and maim him.

When Sir Lucius saw him he said to his Lords:
'This traitor has marched here intent on treason!
He has the city sealed off on several sides
and the crags and chasms are crawling with his men.
There is no way out, and no other option

The Romans encounter the British

but to fight our foe, since we can never flee.'
Then rapidly that ruler arranged his ranks,
rallied his Romans and his royal knights,
and directed the Viscount of Rome to the vanguard
with valiant knights of Viterbo and Venice,
then dressed the pole with the dreaded golden dragon
with eagles all over and adorned with sable.
Wine was drawn, and they drank their draught,
dukes and nobles and newly dubbed knights;
amid dancing Dutchmen and the droning of pipes
every dell in that dale echoed with the din.

Then Sir Lucius spoke loudly with lordly words:
'Think of your fine and famous forebears,
and the ravagers of Rome who reigned with those lords,
whose ranks overran every ruler on earth,
who conquered all Christendom through armed combat,
gaining new ground with every glorious victory;
in seven winters they wore down the Saracens
in every place from Port Jaffa to Paradise Gates.
If a region has its rebel we reckon it nothing,
and by right and reason such radicals are restrained.
So we gird our loins and delay no longer;
for undoubtedly by dusk this day shall be ours.'

As these words were spoken, the Welsh King himself
became aware of this warrior who had warred with his
    knights;
and bravely in the valley he voiced his invective:
'Viscount of Valence, envier of endeavours,

Lucius addresses his army

events at Viterbo shall be avenged, and unvanquished
I shall fight on this field and never take flight.'

    Then the Viscount, with valour, and in noble voice
advanced from the vanguard, venturing on horseback,
sporting a strong shield trimmed with sable
depicting a bloated and dreadful dragon
devouring a dolphin of doleful features,
a certain sign of our Sovereign's destruction,
swept to his death by the slashing of swords,
for when the dragon is flown, death surely follows.

    Then our leader, Valiant, levelled his lance
and with unerring accuracy caught his enemy exactly,
spiking him through the small ribs a span above the waist
so steel plate and spleen were skewered on the spear.
Blood spurted and splurged as the horse sprang about,
then he sprawled lifeless and spoke no longer.
And so Sir Valiant was vindicated and kept his vow,
vanquishing that Viscount who was vaunted as a victor.

    Then Sir Ewain Fitz Urien charged in eagerly,
approaching the Emperor to prise away the eagle;
through his gaggle of guardsmen he quickly galloped,
drew his sword and with spirits soaring
seized it swiftly and then sped away,
returning with the raptor raised in his fist
and falling in with his fellows on his own front line.

    Now Sir Lancelot made ready then rode in rapidly

at Sir Lucius the lord, and a gruesome blow he landed:
his point pierced the plate and also the chain-mail
so the proud pennant impaled in his stomach
and the head stuck out behind by half a foot.
Through hauberk and hip went the hefty weapon
so horse and horseman were hurled to the ground,
then he struck down a standard and steered back to his
    company.

    'I like it,' said Sir Lot, 'that those lords are delivered.
If my lord will allow, the next lot shall be mine!
My name will mean nothing, either now or tomorrow,
unless they leap from life who mass there on that land.'
He straightened in his stirrups and strained his bridle,
went storming into battle on his stunning steed,
engaged with a giant and jagged him right through.
Then jollily that gentle knight out-jousted another,
cut a wide swathe as he scythed down warriors,
woefully wounding those who stood in his way.
He fought through the fray for a furlong's length,
felled many in the field with the force of his weapon,
and had victory in vanquishing valiant knights,
stampeding through the dale then withdrawing as he pleased.

    Thereafter the bold bowmen of Britain
fought with foot-soldiers from foreign lands;
their well-fletched arrows flew at the foe,
piercing the fine mail as far as the feathers.
Such fighting did fearful harm to the flesh,
and arrows flashed from afar into the flanks of the steeds.

Battle commences

In return the Dutchmen dealt out their darts,
and their sharp missiles shattered the shields;
the bolts from their crossbows were so cruelly quick
they sliced the bodies of our brothers before they could blink.
So much did they shrink from the shooting of those shafts
that the scores of defenders on the front line scattered.
Great warhorses bucked then bounded into battle,
and in no time hundreds lay heaped on the heath.
Then hastily the high-born and the heathens and others
hurdled the heads of the dead to do harm.
Those giants at the front, engendered by fiends,
enjoined with Sir Jonathal and his gentle knights,
and with hard steel clubs they clattered at helmets,
crushing down crests and crashing through brains,
slaying infantry and armoured horses,
chopping down chevaliers on chalk-white chargers.
Neither steel or steed could stand against them
as they astounded and struck at our stout defenders,
till the Conqueror came with his keen knights,
and with cruel countenance cried aloud:
'I trust no Briton will be troubled by this trifle,
by bare-legged boys who have blundered into battle.'
He flourished Excalibur, all flashing and flaring,
and galloped to Golapas who had grieved him the most,
and cleaved him cleanly in two at the knees:
'Come down,' said the King, 'and call to your comrades.
You're too high by half I have to tell you;
with our Saviour's help you shall soon be handsomer!'
With his steel sword he swished off his head.
Sternly in the struggle he struck another,

Arthur rides into battle

then set upon several with his stout knights,
and did not cease until sixty were seen off.
And so at this juncture the giants were out-jousted,
slain in the assault by steadfast knights.

Then the Romans and the ranks of the Round Table
regrouped and rearranged, rearguard and others,
and with huge war-weapons they hammered helmets,
striking through strong mail with sturdy weapons.
They gave no ground, those grand warriors,
then with lances stormed in on steel-grey steeds,
fighting frenziedly with flashing spears,
shearing off gold adornments which decorated the shields.
So many fighters were felled on the field
that every tributary through the trees was a torrent of red,
and swathes of green sward were swiftly bloodied.
Swords split in half, and ailing horsemen
slew about in the saddles of stampeding steeds.
Admirable men, all maimed and mauled,
filthy hair framing once-fair features,
were trodden and trampled by trundling horses,
the fairest on earth that were ever formed;
for as far as a furlong a thousand lay felled.

By now the Romans were reeling rather,
and in dread delayed no longer in withdrawing.
Our powerful prince pursued them promptly,
pouncing on their proudest with impressive knights:
Sir Kay, Sir Clegis and Sir Cleremond the noble
encountered them at the cliff with accomplished fighters,

The Romans are pushed back

sparred wildly in the woods, sparing no weapon,
felling fully five hundred in the first attack.
And when their troops noticed how our knights had trapped
   them,
despite being fewer, they were forced to regroup,
and barged into battle, brandishing their spears,
clashing with France's foremost fighters.
Then keen Sir Kay made ready and rode,
went challenging on his charger to chase down a king,
and landed his lance from Lithuania in his side
so that spleen and lungs were skewered on the spear;
with a shudder the shaft pierced the shining knight,
shooting through his shield, shoving through his body.
But as Kay drove forward, he was caught unfairly
by a lily-livered knight of royal lands;
as he tried to turn the traitor hit him,
first in the loins, then further through the flank;
the brutal lance buried into his bowels,
burst them in the brawl, then broke in the middle.
Sir Kay knew well from that cruel wound
that the dint was his undoing and death would follow.
Then he rallied himself and rode at their ranks,
advancing on that villain in search of vengeance.
'Take care, coward,' he called towards him,
then cleaved him cleanly, sundered him with his sword.
'Had my deathblow been dealt with an honest hand,
then by God in heaven, I would grant you forgiveness.'

    He went to his wise King and greeted him worthily:
'I am grievously wounded and my grave awaits.

               Sir Kay is mortally wounded

Work at your duty as the world would wish it
and bring me to burial – I bid nothing more.
Greet my lady Queen, if luck allows your life,
and those beauteous ladies belonging to her bower.
And my worthy wife, who never wronged me,
implore her to plead for my soul in her prayers.'

The King's confessor came with Christ in his hands
to console the knight and absolve him of sin.
And with a noble heart the knight knelt,
to receive his Creator, who comforts us all.
Then the King howled with great hurt in his heart,
and rode into the rout to wreak his revenge.
He ploughed through the pack, and met with a prince
who was heir of Egypt in those eastern marches,
and with Excalibur clinically cleaved him in half,
sliced that soldier, even split the saddle,
so the steed's back was strewn with his bowels.
Savage in his sorrow he sought out another:
through the abdomen of one who had angered him hugely
he tilted and tore him in two through his mail,
so half of that hostile lay heaped on the earth
and the other half rode onward still seated on his horse.
From that hurt, I assume, he will struggle to heal!
Wielding his weapon he wiped out defenders,
shredding men in their shimmering suits,
bringing down banners and obliterating shields,
brutal in his rage with his burnished blade.
Wrathfully he writhed and by force of will
he assaulted soldiers and assailed knights,

Arthur's grief and fury

went thrashing in the thick of it thirteen times,
pressed hard in the throng and thrust straight through.

Then good Sir Gawain with gracious knights
advanced in the vanguard by the verge of the wood,
and as he looked saw Sir Lucius lying in wait
with lords and liegemen loyal to his cause.
Then eagerly the Emperor quickly asked:
'Are you wanting work for your weapon, Gawain?
I sense from your unease that you seek out sorrow.
I shall wreck you, you wretch, for the boldness of your
    bragging.'
He unleashed a long sword and lashed out swiftly,
lunging at Sir Lionel and with a lusty blow
hitting hard at his head, hacking open his helmet
and splitting his skull to a span's depth.
Then he launched at our brothers like a born leader,
wounding our worthy and noble warriors,
fencing with Florent, the finest of our swordsmen,
till foaming blood flowed across his fist.

Then the routed Romans revived and rallied,
scattering our ranks on their rested steeds;
cheered that their chief was so ruthless in his challenge
they chased and chopped down our chivalrous knights.
Sir Bedivere was pierced, punctured at the breast
by a huge weapon, wide at the hilt,
struck through the heart by the stropped steel,
and was hurled to the earth; such heavy sorrow.

Sir Lionel and Sir Bedivere are slain

Then the Conqueror, noticing, came countering with
   numbers
to rescue the royal men of the Round Table
and finish the Emperor if fortune ran fair.
They headed for the eagle; 'Arthur' they hollered.
Eagerly the Emperor lashed out at Arthur,
caught him with a cross-stroke and cracked his visor;
the naked sword swung swiftly at his nose
so the blood of the King streamed brightly on his breast
and ran red on his shield and shimmering armour.
Our bold King spun about with the sparkling bridle
and rode within reach to run him through,
piercing mail and man with his mighty sword,
opening him slantwise from his Adam's apple.
So ended the Emperor at Arthur's hands,
and his fellows and friends looked on afraid.

Now the few that were left went fleeing to the forest
by the fresh streams, out of fear of our folk,
and the cream of our army on iron-grey horses
followed those who tasted fear for the very first time.
Then the crowned Conqueror called to his comrade:
'Cousin of Cornwall, oversee this decree:
that no captain be captured and kept for silver
till Sir Kay's vile killing is viciously avenged.'

      'No,' cried Sir Cador, 'so Christ help me.
No kaiser or king under Christ's reign
will escape cold death by the craft of my hands.'

Then chieftains could be witnessed on chalk-white chargers
chasing and chopping down chivalrous chevaliers,
regal Romans and royal kings,
their ribs ripped apart by ripe steel.
Brains burst through their burnished helmets,
battered by blade on those broad fields.
They hewed down heathens with hilted swords
with a host of hundreds by the edge of the holt.
No silver could save them or secure their souls,
not sultan nor Saracen nor senator of Rome.

Then together the Round Table rallied and regrouped
by the fine river that flowed so fair,
stopped and took stock by those pleasant streams,
in the flatlands by the foreshore, that courageous force.
Then they cantered to the encampment to claim what they pleased:
camels and crocodiles and crammed coffers,
hackneys and asses and armoured horses,
the marquees and canopies of heathen kings.
They led away dromedaries of different lords,
and milk-white mules and many marvellous beasts,
Arab horses and imperious elephants
that issued from the Orient with lords of high office.

But in the aftermath Sir Arthur went at once
with an escort of honourable allies to the Emperor,
then his lords lifted his body lovingly
and bore him to a bed in the Sovereign's own suite.
Then with haste the heralds, at their lord's behest,
went hunting for heathens lying fallen on the heath,

The enemy camp is plundered

the Sultan of Syria and his sworn kings,
sixty of Rome's most celebrated senators.
They laid out and anointed the noble kings,
lapped them in sixty loops of choice linen
then lagged them with lead, to preserve them longer
and to keep, if they could, the corpses from decaying
before arriving in Rome enclosed in a casket,
with banners above and badges below,
announcing as they went so all knights would know
each king by his colours and the country of his crown.

Subsequently on the second day soon after dawn
two senators with their manly soldiers emerged
from the heath's edge, without helmet or hood,
in bare feet across the sward with their swanky swords,
bowing to King Arthur and offering their hilts,
to be hanged or beheaded or hold onto their lives.
They knelt before the Conqueror in nothing but their kirtles
then sheepishly whispered these wary words:
'Two senators we are, your subjects of Rome,
who have saved our skins by these salty streams
by cowering in the copse with the help of Christ.
As our Sovereign lord we beseech your leniency:
allow us, if you will, our lives and limbs,
for His love, who loans you your lordship on this earth.'

'By my grace,' said the good King, 'I hereby grant you
your lives and limbs and permission to leave,
providing you present my proclamation to Rome,
this charge which I shall lay before my chief lords.'

Roman corpses are sealed in coffins

'Yes,' said the senators, 'we shall certainly ensure
that this deed shall be done, we swear it our duty.
No fellow on earth shall defy or deflect us,
be they pope or potentate or noble prince;
on pain of death neither duke nor peer
shall delay us from relaying every letter you pronounce.'

The British bannerets brought them to the tents
where barbers stood by with basins at the ready.
With warm water they wetted them at once
and in suitable style they shaved them to the scalp
to mark those Romans as surrendered men,
and by showing them shorn bring shame upon Rome.
Then quickly they coupled the caskets to the camels:
the highborn went by ass and Arabian horse
and the Emperor himself lay alone and aloft,
born upon an elephant with the eagle flying over.
The King assigned the coffins to the captives
then had his say to all within hearing:
'Here are your coffers to haul across the Alps,
crammed with the measure of money you so craved,
the taxes and tributes of two hundred winters
that were lost to our heart in our ancestor's era.
Say to what senator oversees the city
that I send this sum to assess as he likes.
Bid him never be so brazen while my blood rules these borders
to make an enemy of himself anywhere in this empire
or to claim entitlement to tribute or tax,
or while my time lasts I shall treat him to such treasure.'

Arthur sends the coffins to Rome

So they raced to Rome by the readiest route,
swung the bells of the Capitol to summon citizens
and all the senators and monsignors belonging to that city.
They handed over their cargo, coffins and otherwise,
as the Conqueror had decreed with his cruel words.
'We have travelled on trust to bring you this tribute,
all the rents and revenues from ten score winters
from England and Ireland and the outer isles
that Arthur in the Occident occupies as his own.
He forbids you such boldness, while his blood holds sway,
to come brawling for Britain and its broad acres
or claim tax or tribute or any such title,
bar for treasure like this load, while his time lasts.
We have fought him in France and foul things have happened,
the flower of our folk are feared fallen,
no chieftains or chevaliers have escaped their charges
and chance has seen them chopped down in the chase.
So stock up and stiffen your walls with stone,
and beware, for you awake a wrathful war.'

So on the first of the month of May it followed
that the true royal King with his Round Table
by the clear running streams on the Cotentin coast
inflicted on the Romans a final defeat.
And after fighting in France and winning the field
and fiercely sending every foeman to his fate,
he announced the burial of his bold knights
who by lance and sword were swept from life.
At Bayonne he buried Sir Bedivere the brave,
and at Caen the corpse of keen Sir Kay,

The dead are delivered to Rome

covered entirely with clear crystals,
for his father had fought and conquered that country.
Then in Burgundy he bided while more knights were buried:
Sir Berade was interred and Bishop Baldwin,
and more good men, as their status demanded.

Then afterwards, King Arthur, in early autumn
entered into Germany with his army arrayed;
in Luxembourg he lingered while the injured were healed,
the rightful lord, surrounded by his liegemen.
Then on St Christopher's Day he convened a council
with kings and captains and clerks and others,
and instructed them to turn their intelligent minds
to conquering by combat that country he claimed.
Then the courteous King, courageous and noble,
declared to his council these well-chosen words:
'Enclosed by cliffs in this countryside lives a knight
whose encounter I covet on account of his fame:
the Lord of Lorraine – I shall let it be known.
And they say that the acres he owns are most handsome.
I shall divide and dole out that duchy as I please
and deal with the Duke as destiny allows.
That traitor has been rebel to my Round Table,
always running riot with Romans through my lands.
Readily we shall reckon, if reason has its day,
who has right to those rents and revenues, by Christ!
Then we leave for Lombardy, lovely to the eye,
where I shall lay down laws that will last for ever,
and take on those truculent Tuscan tyrants
and make treaties with their lay lords, which shall last out my time.

Arthur declares war on Lorraine

I shall lend protection to all the Pope's lands
and display to everyone my pennant of peace.
It is folly to offend our Father under God,
or Peter or Paul, those apostles of Rome.
If we follow our faith we fare all the better;
while I have power to pray, our Church is not imperilled.'

Without further speech they spurred on at speed,
those manly knights, to the marches of Metz,
the city where that sovereign lord held sway,
which was as lauded in Lorraine as London is here.
The King forged forwards on his fine steed
with Ferrar and Ferraunt and four other knights;
the seven of them circled the city walls
seeking the best site to set up their siege engines.
Those barricaded within bent back their bows,
and with fearsome faces let fly at our King,
arbalesters aiming their arrows at bold Arthur
to hurt him or his horse with their heinous weapons.
But the King shrugged off those shafts, wouldn't call for a shield,
showed himself, unshrinking, in his shining gear,
lingering and at ease, looking at his leisure
over the wall to where those warriors might be weakest.

'Sir,' said Ferrar, 'you flirt with folly
in nearing those walls so noticeably noble,
coming singly to the city suited only in a surcoat;
such an exhibition might heap harm on us all.
Let's make haste from here before some horror happens,
for if they hit you or your horse we are harmed for ever.'

The British march on the city of Metz

'If you worry,' said the royal one, 'then ride at the rear,
lest they waste you at once with their unwelcome weapons.
It's all that I expected: you are but an infant,
and would be frightened by a fly if it landed on your flesh.
I feel no fear, may God be my friend.
If such groundlings are aggrieved I grimace but little;
they fritter their arrows by firing at my fame.
They shall want for weaponry, on that I wager my head.
My Lord would not allow any knave to have luck
in killing a crowned king with chrism anointed.'

First a vanguard of violent knights made their visit
with army battalions hollering behind,
and fierce foragers, fighting on all fronts,
came storming in on their steel-grey steeds,
riding in array, the reliable allies
of the renowned ranks of the Round Table.
All the faithful men of France followed afterwards,
their frontlines well equipped as they flocked towards the field.
Then knights manoeuvred their mounts to formation
to show off the sheen of their shining apparel,
arranged for battle with banners raised,
shouldering their shields, their helmets shimmering,
pennons and pennants of princes' arms
studded with pearls and precious stones;
light-flashing lances and glittering gear
glared and gleamed and glinted to all sides.
Those superior riders spurred on their steeds,
descended on the city from several sides,
and swiftly they swept the surrounding suburbs,

Metz is attacked

bringing out the bowmen and brawling a little,
scuffling and scaring the shield-men and scouts,
breaking through barricades with their bright weapons,
battering the barbican and reaching the bridge;
had the garrison's great gates not held good
the city would have fallen to their unfailing force.

Then our bold battlers pulled back and drew breath
in dread that the drawbridge might dash them to pieces.
They went then to the camp where the King waited
with his stalwart knights saddled in their steeds.
When the Sovereign was settled, sites were identified
and pavilions of silk were pitched for the siege.
There they lodged like lords, resting as they liked,
watching every ward as to how the war went,
seeing their siege-engines set in place.

On Sunday, when the sun had spread through the land,
the King called to Florent, that flower among knights:
'Our Frenchmen are enfeebled, I should have guessed this
    would follow,
for these folk are foreigners in these far-flung fields
and long for the food and fare of their liking.
There are fine forests here to every flank,
to which our foes have fled, where beasts roam free.
Go forth to the fells and forage through the mountains,
Sir Ferraunt and Sir Floridas shall follow in your footsteps.
Our men fall faint: refresh us with flesh
that feeds in the forests on the fruits of the earth.
Sir Gawain himself will join you on your journey,

Arthur appoints a foraging party

that warden so worthy, as befits him so well,
and those well-honoured knights Sir Wichard and Sir Walter,
with the wisest men of the western marches,
Sir Clegis, Sir Claribald, Sir Cleremond the noble,
and Cardiff's high chieftain, copiously equipped.
Go now, warn the watchmen, Gawain and all others,
and wend your way without further words.'

    They went forward to the forest, those fearless men at arms,
eagerly they entered those painted uplands,
through valleys and vales towards vaulting hills,
through holts and hoar-woods grey with hazel,
by marsh and mossy morass to the mountains,
to where morning mist slept on the meadow,
where scythed hay lay strewn and un-stacked,
swept down in swathes among sweet flowers.
They stepped out of their stirrups and grazed their steeds
as the sun ascended, and songbirds sang
to the miracle of morning, like messengers of our Deity
bringing solace to all sinners who see it on earth.

    Then worthy Sir Gawain wandered off alone,
as was his way, that seeker of wonders,
when he became aware of a well-armed warrior
grazing his warhorse between water and woods,
garbed in gear that was gleaming to the eye,
embracing a bright shield, on a beautiful horse,
with no servants at his side but a young squire
saddled on a steed and carrying his spear.
On his glittering gold shield stood three sable greyhounds,

Gawain encounters a foreign knight

with chokers and chains in chalk-white silver,
and gilding all was a glimmering garnet:
he was a chief amongst chieftains, a challenge for anyone.

Sir Gawain watched him, welcomed the sight,
then gripped hold of his great spear, grabbing it from his
    groom,
stampeded through the stream on his sturdy steed,
and stomped towards that knight with a show of strength,
eagerly crying out 'Arthur', in English.
The other man angrily answered in an instant
in the language of Lorraine, and in a loud voice
that men might listen to a mile away at least.
'What do you mean, mercenary, by rushing up so manfully?
Here you'll profit no plunder, parade as you please.
Unless you battle better and beat me in combat
you shall be my prisoner, for all your proud preening.'

'Sir,' said Sir Gawain, 'so help me God,
such mealy-mouth men don't bother me for a moment.
If you prepare to fight expect pain and peril
before you break from this grove, for all your bluster and
    bleating.'

Then they levelled their lances, those lordly knights,
and spurred in at full speed on their steel-grey steeds,
striking freely with all the strength they could summon
until both spear-shafts shuddered and shattered;
through shields they shot and sheered through chain-mail,
spiking shoulders to the depth of a span.

Gawain lays down a challenge

So in worthy engagement both warriors were wounded,
but till their anger was exhausted they would never give in.
They grabbed at their reins and rode once again,
readily those swift men slashed with their swords,
hitting out at heads with hearty blows,
hewing through hauberks with their heavy weapons.
Stoutly they struck, those stern knights,
stabbing at the stomach with steel points,
fencing and flourishing with flashing blades
until flickering fire-sparks fizzed from their helmets.

Then Sir Gawain was aggrieved and greatly angered.
With his good sword Galuth he struck grievously,
cleaving the knight's shield cleanly in half
so who looked to the left when his horse leapt up
might see his liver by the light of the sun.
Then the warrior groaned, overwhelmed by his wounds,
yet he slashed at Sir Gawain as he swept by his side,
catching him slantwise with a savage slice,
hacking his enamelled ailette in half,
hitting at his armoured upper arm-guard
so the keen edge hived it off at the elbow
by the armoured forearm which was hemmed with argent.
Through a double vesture of invaluable velvet
he had severed a vein with his venomous sword
which bled so thoroughly that his thoughts became blurred,
and his visor and face-guard and all his fine garb
were spotted and spattered with his brave blood.

Then the tyrant rapidly turned his reins,

Both knights are wounded

and talked without tenderness, saying, 'You are touched!
We must bandage your cuts before your colour turns bland!
All the surgeons in Britain could not staunch that blood,
for who is bitten by this blade shall bleed without end.'

'In truth,' said Gawain, 'you trouble me but a trifle.
You intend to terrify me with your tall words,
trusting that your talk sends a tremor though my heart;
but harm shall unhinge you before you pass from here
unless you say out loud, delaying no longer,
what might staunch this blood which streams so briskly.'

'I will speak to you solemnly, swearing my truth,
for no surgeon of Salerno could save you more successfully,
on condition you allow me confession to your Christ,
to absolve me of sin before going to my grave.'

'Yes,' said Sir Gawain, 'so help me God,
I will grant you such grace, though you have grieved me greatly,
if you tell me honestly the object of your errand,
a solitary, single knight, by himself alone,
and what religion you believe in, let the truth be told,
and what land calls you lord, and what allegiance you hold.'

'My name is Sir Priamus, my father is a prince,
praised in his province by proven kings;
in Rome where he reigns he is spoken of as royalty.
But to Rome he was a rebel, and wrestled for its lands,
waging war for many a long winter
by wisdom and wit and warrior-like force,

95   *Sir Priamus reveals his identity*

and by worthy means he made himself mighty.
He is of Alexander's kin, overlord of kings,
and Hector of Troy was grandfather to his uncle.
Such are the clans and the kin that I come from:
from Judas and Joshua, both gentle knights.
I am his heir apparent, his eldest offspring;
of Alexandria and Africa and all those outer empires
I own them all and hold power over each;
from all the principal cities and peoples in those parts
both territory and treasure shall be mine to take,
plus taxes and tributes while my time lasts.
But while I lodged at home, so haughty was my heart
that none below heaven came higher than my hip,
so I was sent on this sortie with seven score knights,
with my father's assent, to experience this insurgence,
and my pride is punctured, for I am shamefully overpowered,
and by effort of arms I am harmed for ever.
So now I have informed you of my family and forbears,
will you, out of knighthood, let me know your name?'

    'By Christ,' Gawain announced, 'I never was a knight,
but a servant in the quarters of the esteemed Conqueror,
working at his wardrobe for long years of winter
on the full armoured suit he preferred for fighting.
And I pitched and prepared his private pavilions,
and dressed his dukes and earls in their doublets,
and Arthur also in his padded under-jacket
that he has worn in war all these eight winters.
He made me yeoman at Yuletide and yielded to me gifts:
a hundred pounds, and a horse, and heavy armour.'

                                       Gawain claims to be a servant

'Should I serve that Sovereign if my health is restored
then help me with haste, I don't hesitate to say so!
If his nobodies are like you then his knights must be noble!
No king under Christ could challenge him in conflict.
He will be heir to Alexander to whom the whole earth bowed,
and more able even than Hector of Troy.
Now, on the holy oil by which you were anointed,
let me know for certain – are you knight or knave?'

'My name is Sir Gawain, I grant you that knowledge,
cousin to the Conqueror, who acclaims me as his kin,
enrolled in his records as a knight of his company,
and rated richest of the Round Table.
I am a duke of the duchy, whom he dubbed by his own hands,
an honour witnessed by his well-loved warriors.
Grudge it not, good sir, that such grace is mine –
to be gifted such fortune is by God's agreement.'

'By Peter,' cried Priamus, 'it pleases me more
than if I were prince of Paris or Provence.
For I would sooner you secretly stabbed me to the heart
than have some commonplace person profit such a prize.
But there is, close at hand, holed up in the holts,
a huge army – take heed of that host:
the bold Duke of Lorraine and his loyal braves,
Dauphiné's doughtiest and many Dutchmen,
those respected leaders the Lords of Lombardy,
the garrison of Mount St Gothard, splendidly garbed,
the warriors of Westphalia, worthy soldiers,
and from Saxony and Syria Saracens in their scores.

Gawain reveals his true status

They are named on the rolls and are known to number
sixty thousand and ten, it is true, of the toughest.
Unless you hurry from this heath we shall both come to harm,
and if my healing is not hastened I shall never more be whole.
Tell your henchman to hold from sounding his horn
or expect to be swiftly sliced to pieces.
For they are my retinue, who ride at my rule,
and no worthier warriors hold sway in this world.
If you are found by that force you shall journey no further,
and shall never be ransomed for all the riches in man's reach.'

    So Sir Gawain headed out of harm's way
with that honourable knight who was horribly injured,
and came to the mountains where our company were camped,
grazing their steeds on the grassy slopes,
lords leaning and lying on their shining shields,
and their love of birdsong brought their laughter aloft,
of the lark and the linnet and their lovely tunes.
And some slipped into sleep, soothed by those creatures
singing of the season in the sun-kissed woods,
lulled by the music which murmured through the land.
Then Sir Wichard was aware that their warlord was wounded,
and went to him weeping and wringing his hands;
yes, Sir Wichard, and Sir Walter, those worthy men at arms,
worried for their knight, walked straight toward him,
met him in the middle and thought it a marvel
that he had mastered that man of such mighty strength.
Yet all the wealth in the world would not mend their woe:
'All our worth on this earth is gone well away.'

Priamus tells of an enemy presence

'Grieve not,' said Gawain, 'for God in heaven's love,
for this harm is but gossamer, an honour for an earl.
Though my shield was shot through and my shoulder slashed
and hurt issues from the movement of my injured arm,
this prisoner, Priamus, who has perilous wounds,
insists that he has salves which will save us both.'

Those stern knights stepped up to assist him from his
    stirrups,
and he alighted like a lord, pulling the bridle loose,
letting his horse go free to feed from the flowers.
He drew off his helmet and climbed out of his armour,
then leant on his great shield and bent low to the ground;
that bold man's body was drained of all its blood.
Then the peerless knights pressed towards Sir Priamus,
tenderly helped him from his horse in their arms
and afterwards took off his helmet and hauberk,
then with haste before his hurt caused his heart to seize
they lowered him to the lawn, lightened of his gear,
and he laid out full length, which allowed him some comfort.
A vial of fine gold they found at his girdle,
filled with the waters of the four wells
that flow from Paradise when the flood rises
which nourishes the fruit that feeds us as it falls.
He whose severed sinews are rubbed with that salve
shall be fitter than a fish within four hours.
They unclothed the bodies with their clean bare hands
and with clear water a knight cleaned their cuts,
cooling them and comforting their hearts with kindness.
And when the cuts were cleansed they covered them up,

Both knights receive treatment for their wounds

then broke open barrels and brought them wine
and roast meat and brawn and the very best bread,
and after they had eaten they were armed once more.

Then, 'Aux Arms!' those adventuring heroes cried out,
and with a clarion call that company of men
held council together to discuss their case.
'Yonder lies an army of heavily armed enemies,
the cruellest in combat that exists under Christ;
that host is arrayed in the oak wood there,
determined troops from the outlying territories,
so Sir Priamus promises, so help us St Peter.'
'Up, men,' said Gawain, 'and ask in your heart:
who shall go to that grove and greet those lords;
if we return empty-handed then Arthur will be angry
and say we are timorous, troubled by mere trifles.
But fortune finds us with none other but Sir Florent,
the flower of all France who never fled in battle.
He was chosen and charged in the chamber of the King
as chieftain of this challenge, by noble chevaliers.
If he fights or flees, we shall follow him to the end,
and I shall never forsake him out of fear of that foe.'

'Sir,' said Sir Florent, 'you speak fairly,
yet I am but an infant, inexperienced in arms;
if folly befalls us the fault shall be ours;
we shall be forced from France to live as exiles forever.
Without offence to your worthiness, my wit is feeble:
you are the leading lord – allow things as you like.'

Gawain urges his comrades to fight

'You are only five hundred,' Sir Priamus argued,
'which is far too few to fight with them all,
and your skivvies and skivers shall scarcely be of use,
and will turn tail and run for all their tall talk.
I recommend you use your minds, as military men,
and get cleanly and cleverly clear of this place.'

'Granted,' said Sir Gawain, 'but so help me God,
here are worthy warriors who deserve some reward,
the keenest knights of the King's chamber.
With goblet in gauntlet they have spoken great words,
and today will prove who shall profit the prize.'

Now the foragers of the force headed towards the forest,
going forwards through the fields, first on horseback then on foot;
then hunting down their prey like princely men at arms
came Florent and Floridas with five score knights,
following the men who had forged through the firth,
fast on their mounts to fall upon the foe.
But hurtling on our folk came fully five hundred
ferocious fighters on fresh horses,
one Sir Ferrant at the front on a fine steed,
from a Famagustan family, the Fiend was his father.
He flew at Sir Florent and shouted foul words:
'Why flee, false knight? The Fiend have thy soul.'
Then Sir Florent was inflamed and made ready to fight;
on Fawnell of Friesland he charged at Ferrant,
yanked at the reins of that right royal horse,
and raced into the rout, not resting for a second.
Fully in the forehead he fixed his enemy,

British knights engage the forces of Lorraine

disfiguring his face with his fierce weapon;
through his head and helmet he hammered his brain,
breaking the neck-stem and stopping his breath.

His cousin who looked on cried out loudly,
'You have killed cold-dead the king of all knights,
who flourished in the field in fifteen realms
never finding a foe to match him in a fight.
You shall die for this deed with my dreaded weapon,
and your craven company who cower in those woods.'

'Fie,' called Sir Floridas, 'you defiant wretch,
do you think we are shocked by a shallow-mouthed shrew?'
And our knight, with his sword, as he swept by the insurgent
left the flesh of his flank cut open and flapping
so his gizzards and the filthy gore of his guts
lay foul among the feet of his foal when he galloped.

Then in rode a knight, rushing to his rescue.
It was Raynald of Rhodes, a rebel to Christ,
perverted by those pagans who persecute Christians.
He pressed in proudly in the chase for his prey;
in Prussia he had won himself praise and prestige,
so he barged into battle as bold as brass.
But Sir Richard, a true knight of the Round Table
on a sterling stallion came strongly against him.
Through a round, red shield he rammed his weapon
so the heat-tempered spear went spiking through his heart.
He slewed about in his saddle then slumped to the earth,
and roared rudely, but rode no more.

Knights in battle

Now all the hearty and unhurt of the five hundred
fell on Sir Florent and his five score knights
between a bog and a brook on a level strip of land,
so our forces regrouped to face their foe.
Then long and loud came the cry 'Lorraine'
as lords rushed forward with long, levelled lances,
and 'Arthur' on our side when harm was at hand.

  Then Sir Florent and Sir Floridas set their spears
    forwards
and rushed at their rivals, sending fear through their ranks,
felling five at the front on their first charge
and a fair few more before pressing further.
They breached braided armour and broke bright shields,
battering and beating the best who opposed them.
All the rulers of those ranks went riding away,
roundly rousted by those royal knights.

  When Sir Priamus the prince perceived the proceedings
he felt pity in his heart not to enter the action,
so went to Gawain and gave him these words:
'Your prized men are pressed very hard by their prey;
the Saracens are swarming, more than seven hundred
of the Sultan's soldiers from assorted lands.
Would you suffer me, sir, for the sake of your Christ,
to stand at their side with a team of your troops.'

  'I grudge not,' said Gawain, 'that the glory is theirs,
and great gifts will be granted them by their lord.
So let the fierce men of France now confirm their worth:

Priamus offers his support to the British

they have fought no foe for full fifteen winters!
I will not stride to their assistance by half a steed's length
unless sterner opposition come storming to the field.'

Then Gawain was aware at the edge of the woods
that the warriors of Westphalia on worthy mounts
were galloping rapidly where the road runs,
with every weapon, on my oath, that war ever owned.
The Earl of Antele led the vanguard,
with eight thousand knights on either hand,
his bowmen and shield-bearers being bigger in total
than any king had equipped for combat on this earth.

Then the Duke of Lorraine came riding right after,
with double that in Dutchmen who were deemed so mighty,
and pagans from Prussia, those praised horsemen,
pressing proudly forward with Priamus's knights.
Then the Earl of Antele said to Algere his brother:
'I am angered to my heart by Arthur's knights
who so eagerly hurl themselves against our host.
Before the morning bell we will butcher them to a man,
so foolishly have they come to fight us on this field.
If they save their skins it will seem a wonder.
But if they turned and took an alternative track,
returned to their prince and stopped attacking their prey
they might lengthen their lives and lose but a little,
which would lighten my heart, so help me Lord.'

'Sir,' said Sir Algere, 'they are hardly in the habit
of failing in fight. It inflames me all the more

Lorraine himself arrives with reinforcements

that as few as they are, the fairest of our folk
shall fall to their deaths before they flee the field.'

   Then good Sir Gawain, gracious and noble,
in glorious spirit gladdened his great knights:
'Don't shiver at the sight of those shimmering shields
which those empty men flaunt on their fine horses.
Bannerets of Britain, be bold in your hearts.
Do not baulk at those boys in their bright outfits.
We shall obliterate their boasts till they do our bidding,
submissive as a maid in her master's bed.
If we fight without fear the field shall be ours;
the fakers shall fail and falsehoods shall be fractured.
Their folk in the frontline are untested and fragile,
their deity is the Devil and they swear him their duty.
In the venture before us victory shall be ours,
to be valued by the voices of valiant men,
praised by princes in the presence of lords
and loved by ladies in diverse lands.
Not one of our elders ever earned such high honour,
not Unwin or Absalom or any other.
When most in distress we shall pray to Mother Mary,
our Sovereign's saint, whom he trusts most solemnly,
that Queen whose kind-heartedness honours us all.
Who reveres the virgin mother shall never be vanquished!'

   Once this speech was spoken, the sides were only separated
by the length of the field. 'Lorraine!' cried the foe.
And never was a bloodier battle embarked upon,
not even in the epic of Jehosaphat's Vale

Gawain's battle speech

when death brought judgement to Julius and Joatell,
as when royal riders of the Round Table
rushed into the rout on their regimental steeds,
for so speedily did they strike with their tempered spears
that the rogues and rascals ran to the woods
and the court they came from, to be known as cowards.

'By Peter,' said Gawain, 'it gives me great gladness
that those nobodies are gone, who gathered in such number.
I trust now those tinkers will trouble us not a trifle,
for they will hastily hide in the hem of the holt;
there are forty thousand fewer now on that field
than were first counted among their full force.'

Then one Julian of Genoa, a huge giant,
joined battle with Sir Gerard, a justice of Wales;
but in joust he jabbed him through his gyronny shield,
cut open and maimed him through his coat of mail;
joints and splices he sliced and sundered.
On a swift steed he made this sortie,
and the giant was out-jousted, that wandering Jew,
and Gerard was justly joyful in spirit.

Then the horsemen of Genoa hurtled as one,
with five hundred men pressing forward at the front.
A fellow named Sir Frederick and many of his force
came hammering in, hollering eagerly,
to fight with our foragers on the field of battle.
Then the true royals of the Round Table
with great gusto went galloping against them,

The battle rages

though in the melees with their middle-guard they were ill-
    matched.
What a marvel to see such a massing multitude!
Soon in the engagement the Saracens could see
that the Sovereign of Saxony was struggling badly,
his giants being out-jousted by gentle knights
and being jabbed in the heart through their Genoese hauberks.
They whacked through the helmets of those haughty warriors
and sank their hilted swords to their hearts.
Then the renowned ranks of the Round Table
ran down and rived those renegade wretches.
So dukes and earls were dispatched to their death
all the length of the day by dreadful deeds.

Then the prince Sir Priamus in the presence of lords,
went darting to his pennon and publicly commandeered it,
rapidly reversed it and rode away
to the royal troops of the Round Table;
his retinue rushed to join their ranks,
seeing the sign on his shield as their signal.
Like sheep from the fold they streamed from their squadron,
and stood at the side of their lord in the struggle.

Then those warriors duly sent word to the Duke:
'We have served you as soldiers for six years or more,
but we leave you today out of loyalty to our lord,
and will follow him faithfully through far kingdoms.
You defaulted on our fees for these four winters,
you are feeble and false, with nothing but fine words.
Our wages are withheld, so your war is over,

Priamus's men join the British cause

and we may wander where we wish with our heads held high.
We entreat you to settle for a truce without trifling,
or lose ten thousand of your troops at least.'
'*Fy a diables*,' cried the Duke, 'the Devil take your bones.
You dogs hold no dread and will never be a danger.
We shall duel this day by deeds of arms
with my fate and fortune in the hands of fellow knights.
Such mercenaries as you men I mind but a little,
who suddenly and shamefully forsake their leader.'

The Duke and his liegemen delayed no longer;
he drew out a dromedary and with dreaded knights
galloped at Sir Gawain with great numbers
of grim and grievous warriors from Granada.
Those men at the front on their fresh mounts
felled our foragers forty at a time,
who had already faced a force of five hundred –
no wonder, in faith, that they waned and grew faint.
Then Sir Gawain was aggrieved and gripped his spear
and went in again with gallant knights,
ran through the Marquis of Metz as they met,
the fellow who had infuriated him furthest on earth.
And one Chastelayne, a squire of the Sovereign's chamber
and ward to Sir Gawain of the western marches,
chased down Sir Cheldrick, a noble chieftain,
and with a hunting spear he spiked and holed him,
a feat achieved by good fortune in the fight.
But they pursued that squire so he would never escape,
and one Swyan of Sweden, with the edge of his sword,
severed the young noble's spine at his nape.

Chastelayne the squire is killed

He lurched, falling full length on the field,
and died a swift death, his days at an end.

Then Gawain's grey eyes were wet with weeping
because that brave boy was but a beginner in battle;
sadness at his falling filled his face,
and chill tears ran in channels down his cheeks.
'Woe is me,' cried Gawain, 'that my wits were found wanting.
Every penny I possess I promise to stake
in my vow to avenge the villain who wounded him.'
Then dolefully he armed and dashed towards the Duke,
but one Sir Dolphin the Dauntless came driving in;
Sir Gawain spiked him with his grim spear
so the sharpened shaft went shooting to his heart.
Eagerly he hit out and hurt another,
the heathen Hardolf, excellent in arms,
wounding him wickedly right through his windpipe,
and the spear that he held slipped from his hands.
On that slope, some sixty fierce soldiers he slew
by his knightly skills, and they slid to the swamp.
And though Gawain was grieved, he watched and waited,
till he witnessed the one who had wounded the lad,
and swiftly with a sword he swiped him clean through
so he dropped on the field and died where he fell.
Then he rode into the host, hacking through helmets,
riving off rivets and ripping through shields,
causing carnage in the ranks but keeping his course,
rampaging through the rearguard and riding onwards,
then reining back, that right royal battler,
and returning to the ranks of his own Round Table.

Gawain rampages in anger and grief

Then our chivalrous men changed their chargers
and chased and chopped down many noble chieftains,
hitting out heartily at helmets and shields,
hurting and hewing through those heathen knights.
Through kettle-hats they cleaved, cutting to the shoulder –
such a clamour of captains was never heard on earth!
The courteous sons of kings were captured,
and knights of the country, noble of name;
lords of Lorraine and lords of Lombardy
were seized and led in by our loyal soldiers.
Those that fled from the field found better fortune,
for to stay and stage battle would only bring bitter strife.

When Sir Florent had won the field by force,
he foraged still further with five score knights;
their prizes and prisoners were passed down the line
by bowmen and bold soldiers and bearers of shields.
And good Sir Gawain, guiding his knights,
took the least winding way, as his scouts had warned
that he might be greeted by a garrison of great lords
who would grab his goods and work other such grief.
So sentries were installed along the straight, and with stealth
he went along the path until the peril had passed.

When they saw the city which their Sovereign had besieged,
which the same day would be seized by assault,
a herald went ahead at the lord's behest,
home to his lodgings, back from the highlands,
and turned to the tent where the King made his camp
to tell the tale of how they had triumphed.

The British secure victory over Lorraine's army

'All your forces walk free who battled afar.
Sir Florent and Sir Floridas and your noble knights;
fearlessly they have foraged and have fought great numbers,
leaving many of your foe lying felled in the field.
Our worthy warden has served us well,
for today he has gained us glory for all time.
He dealt death to the Dauphin and seized the Duke!
Many honourable enemies were slain by his hand!
Imprisoned as his prizes are princes and earls
of the richest blood to reign in any realm.
All your finest fellows have been favoured by good fortune,
though a child, Chastelayne, by mischance was killed.'
'Herald,' said the King, 'by Him in heaven,
you have healed my heart, and on honour I promise
to pay you a hundred pounds back in Hampton.'

The Sovereign then assembled his knights for assault,
with scaffolds and siege machines to every side,
shifting the shield-bearers to scale the walls,
and a guard stood watch over every armed group.
Then quickly and with courage they cranked back the catapults,
and with payloads in place they pelted and pounded;
hospitals and monasteries they hammered to the earth,
and churches and chapels with their chalk-white paint,
till sturdy stone steeples lay scattered in the streets,
and houses with chimneys and many choice hostelries.
As they pummelled and pulverised the plastered walls
the agony of inhabitants was harrowing to hear.

Then the Duchess herself, with her dutiful damsels,

The siege and bombardment of Metz

and the Countess of Crasine in the company of her maidens,
bowed before the King on the castle's battlements
where he halted on his ornamented armoured horse.
They knew him by his countenance, and cried keenly:
'Worthy King, take kindly to these words!
We beseech you, sir, as Sovereign and lord,
that you save us today, for the sake of your Saviour.
Take pity upon us and make peace with the people,
before the city is razed by this rapid assault.'

   With the lifting of his visor his look was unveiled,
and with a virtuous visage that valiant man
spoke these calm, kind and comforting words:
'No men of mine shall mistreat you, madam.
Peace I pledge you and your peerless maids,
and to children, chaste priests and to chivalrous knights.
But the Duke is in danger, doubt it not a little.
He is due to be undone, dare for nothing else.'

   Then he sent out his senior lords to each station
to cease the assault, for the city was seized.
Through her eldest son she handed over the keys;
the same night, by assent of nobles, came surrender.
The Duke and his lords were delivered to Dover
where he dwelt in doom for the rest of his days.

   Once the King's conquest was beyond question
with the castle secured and cruel, keen fighters
cornered and captured by craft of arms,
then captains and constables declared him their lord.

Metz falls to the British

He devised and dealt out among diverse families
a dowry for the Duchess and her dear children,
and appointed wardens to wield power in those provinces
he had won in war with his worthy knights.
So in Lorraine he loitered, lord over all,
laying down laws in that land as he pleased.
Then on Lammas Day he left for Lucerne,
and lodged there at leisure, taking pleasure as he liked.
There his galleys were gathered in great numbers,
all glittering like glass under green hills,
with canopied cabins for crowned kings
and covers of gold cloth for knights and other company.
Soon they stowed their gear and stabled their steeds
then struck out across the straits into steeper climbs.

Now happy in his heart he hauled his great army
over massive mountains and through marvellous passes.
He wound by Mount St Gothard and won the watchtower,
and in grappling with the garrison inflicted grisly wounds.
As he crested the peak, the King then paused,
and with the entire battalion took in the view,
looking out over Lombardy and declaring loudly:
'I am lord of this lovely land, I believe.'

Then with kings for company they came to Como,
claimed to be the key to both country and coast.
Sir Florent and Sir Floridas went foraging ahead,
with a good five hundred fearless men of France;
with stealth and speed they sought the best route,
then set up an ambush, as suited their aim.

Arthur pushes on to Como

Then soon after sunrise, issuing from the city
came a scourge of scouts, skilful on their mounts;
slyly they scoured the hills for skulkers,
hunting out hiders to head off any harm.
Peasants and shepherds proceeded in their slipstream
bringing pigs to pasture through the proud gates,
and loitering servants laughed out loud
at a wild boar who bolted for the woods.

    Then our ambushers broke out and overran the bridge,
surged into the city bearing their banners,
stabbing and sticking those who stood against them,
destroying four streets forever before stinting.

    Through the far gate fled numberless folk
in fear of Sir Florent and his fierce knights;
they deserted the city and scurried to the forest
with victuals and vessels and valuable vestures.
Above the broad gate a banner was hoisted,
flying there for Sir Florent, who had never felt finer.
The King waited beyond the wall, halting on a hill,
and said, 'I see from that sign that the city is ours.'
Then he arrived and entered, with his army arrayed,
meaning to stay there until morning at most.
And to each of his squadrons he spoke sternly,
that on loss of limb and forfeit of land
no lord or liegeman owing loyalty to himself
should lie with any lady or lovely maiden
or burgess's wife, or worse or better woman,
or mishandle any citizen who inhabited the city.

                                                  Como is taken

Then at Como the Conqueror held his court
in the acclaimed castle with anointed kings,
and calmed the concerned commoners of that region
with comforting well-chosen words of wisdom.
One of their company he declared as his captain,
so the country and his kingship were quickly in accord.

Then the Lord of Milan heard the city was lost,
and ordered his high-ranking lords to Arthur
with sixty steeds saddled with great sums of gold,
and beseeched him, as Sovereign, to show sympathy to the
   people,
and swore to serve as his subject forever,
and loyally give homage for all of his lands,
for Piacenza, Ponte and Potremoli,
and for Pisa and Pavia, and also made pledges
of purple dye and silk and precious stones,
palfreys fit for princes and proven steeds,
and from Milan the amount of a million in gold,
to be offered honourably every Martinmas,
for ever, without asking, for Arthur and his heirs,
in allegiance to Britain for the length of his life.
The King and his council promised him safe conduct,
and he came to Como and acclaimed him as his lord.

Then in time, Arthur turned his attention to Tuscany,
trampled and took those turreted towns,
walloped down walls and wounded knights,
toppling towers and tormenting the locals.
He made worthy widows wail with sorrow,

Milan capitulates

weeping and howling they wrung their hands.
And everywhere in his wake he wasted through war
their wealth and their houses, and awoke their woe.

They spurred on, spread out, spared very little,
plied violence without pity, despoiled the vines,
spent without censure what was saved or stored,
then sped to Spoleto with their countless spears.
Reports of him sprang from Spain to Prussia,
and they spoke in bitter terms of his exorbitant excesses.
Then to Viterbo the valiant man veered on his mount,
and advisedly in that vale allowed his men victuals
of Vernage and other vintages, and baked venison,
with a view to loitering in the viscount's land.
And soon the vanguard were unsaddling their steeds
and resting in Vertennon's vale of many vines.
There the Sovereign was ensconced, consoled in his heart,
waiting to see if any senators sent word,
revelling and carousing with rich wine,
this true royal with his Round Table,
among mirth and melody and many kinds of pleasures;
nowhere on earth was humankind as happy.

On Saturday, at noon, after seven more nights,
the most quick-minded cardinal of the Roman court
came before the conquering King on his knees,
praying for peace, appealing for a promise
to take pity on the Pope, now put under pressure,
seeking a ceasefire for the sake of our Lord
for seven days, so the senate might assemble,

Tuscany is ransacked

then on the subsequent Sunday they would certainly accept
   him
in the city of Rome as their ruler and Sovereign,
and with anointed hands announce him as King,
swear him their lord with his sceptre and sword.
And to uphold the agreement he offered hostages:
eight-score charming and high-bred children,
attired in rich silk from top to toe,
handed over to Arthur and his honourable knights.
So a truce was obtained, and with trumpets blaring
they took to a tent where tables were set.
The King was seated with his comrades at his side,
beneath a silk canopy, satisfied in such company.
The senators were separated and seated apart,
then were solemnly served with succulent food.
The monarch, full of mirth, with merry words,
gave hospitality to those Romans at his royal table,
and was kind enough to comfort the cardinal himself.
Yes, that royal ruler, so the romances tell,
played host to his enemy, honouring them as guests.
And later, when they deemed it their duty to withdraw,
the learned lords took their leave of the King,
seeking to go straight to the city that night,
leaving the hostages in Arthur's hands.

Then the conquering King declared these words:
'Now we revel and we rest, for Rome is ours!
Make our hostages at home, those children of high birth,
and take care of every man who marches at the command
of the Emperor of Germany and everywhere to the east:

The Pope sends word of Rome's submission

we shall be overlord of all that exists on earth!
By Ascension Day we will seize every city
and by Christmas Day will be duly crowned,
to rule as is my right, and hold my Round Table,
with revenues from Rome to be raised as I please,
then sail the great sea with my good soldiers,
in revenge for our Christ who was crucified on the cross.'

      Then the courteous King, as the chronicles record,
went at once to his bed with a happy heart,
and did not dally in undressing and undoing his girdle,
and for lack of sleep slipped swiftly into slumber.
But in the hour after midnight his mood altered,
for as morning drew near he met with a nightmare,
and when that dreadful dream had drawn to its end
he convulsed with violence, convinced he would die.
So he summoned his sages and spoke of his scare:
'In faith, since I was formed, I was never so afraid,
so look to your learning and translate my dream
as I tell it to you now, truthfully and entire.
I believed I was in a wood, wandering alone,
wholly unaware of which way I should walk.
For wolves and wild boars and wicked beasts
prowled that dark place, scavenging for prey;
lions lurked there, licking their lips,
that would love to lap at the blood of my lords.
I fled through that forest towards tall flowers,
to hide in fear of those foul forms,
and emerged in a meadow ringed by mountains,
the most wondrous in the world that a man could witness.

Arthur recounts his nightmare

The enclosure, in its compass, was carpeted over
with clover and cow-grass, evenly clad;
the vale was encircled by silver vines
growing golden grapes that were never greater.
There were arbours to all aspects and trees of every type,
with livestock grazing on the lawns beneath the groves.
Every fruit to be found on the earth flourished there,
borne and nurtured on those noble boughs,
with no trace of tainting dankness or dew,
for in that fine dry heat all flowers grew fair.

'Then down into the dell, descending from the clouds,
came a duchess, exquisitely dressed and adorned,
in a silk surcoat of astonishing colours,
with otter fur flowing as far as the hem
and ladylike lappets a yard in length,
all trimmed and tapered with tassels of gold
and with badges and brooches and buttons and coins.
Her back and her breast were emblazoned all over;
she wore a kell for her hair and a coronet to her head.
And never had such a notable complexion been known.

'And in her white hands she whirled a wheel about,
working it with such wonder that all else was overwhelmed.
Its circle was beset with red gold and royal stones
and arrayed all around with rubies and rich gems.
The spokes were plated with pleats of silver,
their span from the centre being a spear-length at least.
Set on it was a chair of chalk-white silver,
chequered with rubies of quivering colours.

Lady Fortune appears

And around its circumference kings were clinging on,
wearing crowns of pure gold which were cracking apart.
Six of them had suddenly been slung from that seat,
every one of them crying these words as they went:
"I shall rue without rest that I reigned on this wheel.
Such a rich and royal king never ruled upon this earth:
on my mount, with my men, I had nothing more in mind
than to ride and run riot and hold the people to ransom.
In such unseemly pursuits my days were spent,
and for those dire deeds I am damned forever."

    'The first, a small man, had been flung to the floor;
his loins were too lean and loathsome to look upon,
his locks had grown grey and at least a yard long,
he was facially gruesome and physically deformed,
one eye shone like shimmering silver,
the other was more yellow than the yolk of an egg.
"I was lord," said that man, "of unlimited lands,
and every being alive bowed low in allegiance.
But now I have nothing, not a rag for my nakedness,
and am lost without delay – let every man believe me."

    'The second fellow who was soon to follow suit
seemed strong to my sight and a steely man of arms,
but sighed sorrowfully while speaking these words:
"On that seat I once sat as sovereign and lord,
lapped in the arms of loving ladies.
But now my laurels are lost and lie littered for ever."

    'The third man was squat and square at the shoulders,

thirty would have thought hard before throwing him a threat!
His diadem, dotted and adorned with diamonds
and studded with stately stones, had slipped down.
"In different realms I was dreaded in my day,
but am damned to death and eternal doom."

    'The fourth looked a fairer and forceful fighter
whose figure and features were once marvellously formed.
"I was famous, by my faith, when I ruled in foreign fields,
feted in far lands, the flower of all kings.
Now my face is faded and foulness pollutes me;
I lie fallen to the floor, friendless and alone."

    'The fifth looked finer than the rest of those fellows,
a lusty man, and fierce. But he foamed at the lips.
His arms he locked rigid to hang on to the rim,
but he failed and fell and plunged fifty feet.
Then sprang up and sprinted, spreading his arms,
then he spluttered, sprawled among the spear-length spokes:
"I was Sir of all Syria, I alone they served,
the unassailable sovereign of several kings' lands.
Now in solace and sorrow I am suddenly cast down,
and for the sake of my sins that seat is denied me."

    'The sixth had a Psalter, specially bound,
with a silk cover, carefully sewn,
and a harp and a handsling with hard flint-stones,
and the hurt which had harmed him he howled out loud:
"In my day I was deemed, by my deeds of combat,
undoubtedly the doughriest that dwelt upon earth,

Six of he Nine Worthies are flung from the Wheel

but as my strength reached its summit I was slung down the
   slope
by that mild-seeming maiden who moves all men."

    'Two kings were climbing, clambering up the wheel,
coveting and craving the crest of that compass.
"This chair of choice rubies is our challenge now
as the two on earth most intended for the top."
Like children they were chalk-white, their cheeks and all over.
But the chair above them they never achieved.
The furthest looked fatherly with a firm forehead,
of the finest physique that was ever formed,
and his dress was dyed a decorous blue,
fully flourished with gilded fleurs-de-lis.
His companion was clad in a coat of pure silver
with a glorious cross, carved in gold,
and four little crosses to be found by the larger one,
so the king was a Christian, I knew without question.

    'Then I graciously greeted that glittering lady.
She said, "Welcome, worthily, and it is well you are here.
A word to the wise – you should worship my will
more than any hero who was here on earth,
for all your worth as a warrior has been won by me.
To you I have been helpful, and hostile to others,
as you have found, in faith, and so have your fellows,
for I felled Sir Frollo and his fearsome knights,
and made the fruits of France fall freely to your hand.
That you ascend to the seat I shall see to myself,
choose you for the chair before all chieftains in the world."

                                      Arthur is raised to the summit

She lifted me lightly in her ladylike hands,
sat me softly in the seat and presented me with the sceptre,
then with craft and care ran a comb through my hair
until my crimpled locks came curling around my crown.
Then she dressed me in a strikingly adorned diadem
and offered me an orb, studded with rare stones
and enamelled with azure, depicting the earth,
surrounded on all sides by the great salt seas –
the symbol which insisted my sovereignty of the world.
Then she handed me a sword with a highly polished hilt.
"Wield this weapon of mine," said the woman,
"much blood has been spilt at the bite of its blade,
and as you slash and swish it will serve you unswervingly."
Then she left at her leisure, to rest as she liked
in the furlongs of the forest flourished with foliage:
no prince on earth had ever owned such an orchard,
and paradise alone claimed plants so proud.
She bade the boughs bend and bring to my palm
the best that they bore from the highest branches,
and they heeded her orders, every one at once,
all the grove's tallest trees, I tell no untruth.
All that tempting fruit she enticed me to taste.
"Noble sir, make free with these fine fruits,
reach for the ripest and revel in their richness,
and rest, royalty, for Rome is yours,
and readily I shall roll the wheel by its rim
and pour you potent wine into pristine cups."

'Then she went to the well at the wood's border
which brimmed bewilderingly with bounteous wine,

Lady Fortune favours Arthur

and calmly she caught up a cupful and raised it,
and I drank down a toast to that duchess at her telling.
So that lady led me for the length of an hour,
with all the love and delight that a lord could desire.
But at the minute of midday her mood darkened;
she amazed me with words of malice and menace,
and when I begged for fairness her brows became enflamed.
"King, your cries are in vain, by Christ,
for all you love you shall lose, and your life as well.
You have loitered in privilege and pleasure too long."
Then she whirled the wheel about, and under it I went,
so in a moment every muscle in my body was mangled
and my spine was split asunder by the seat.
Ever since this chapter I have shivered with a chill,
and awake I am wearied by the weight of the dream.
I have told of my torment, now interpret as you wish.'

'Sir,' said the sage, 'your good fortune has ceased.
You shall find her your foe, no matter how you fight.
You sway at the summit, I swear it is so,
so challenge as you may, you will never achieve more.
You have shed much blood, butchered many beings,
killed civilians out of vanity through vast kingdoms.
Now shuck off your shame and shape yourself for death.
That dream was your destiny, doubt it if you dare,
but you shall fall with great force within five winters.
Found abbeys in France – its fortunes are yours –
to Frollo and Ferrant and their fierce knights
whom you uncouthly cut down in that same country.
And heed in your heart what happened to those kings

Arthur is thrown from the Wheel

who were called Conquerors and crowned on this earth.
The most ancient was Alexander, bowed to by all,
then Hector of Troy, that hero of high honour.
The third Julius Caesar, judged a just warrior,
in battle the boldest said his brothers in arms.
The fourth was Sir Judas, a jouster and true gentleman,
and a masterful Maccabee of mighty strength.
Joshua who brought joy to Jerusalem's host
was the fifth, a fair and flawless knight.
David was the sixth, spoken of by sovereigns
as most dutiful and diligent of the knights to be dubbed,
for by skill of his hand he slew with a sling
that hulk Goliath, the most awesome on earth,
then passed his days patiently composing
all the psalms in the psalter with sacred words.
Of those two kings who clambered and climbed,
the first shall be Charlemagne, son of the French sovereign,
merciless and mighty, he shall be made a Conqueror,
capturing countless countries by combat.
He shall secure the crown worn by Christ himself,
and the lance that speared harm into our Lord's heart
while crucified on the cross; and those cruel nails
he will seek and keep safe for the sake of all Christians.
The second shall be Godfrey, who in the service of God
shall bring vengeance on Good Friday with his valiant
    fighters.
By leave of his father he shall be lord of Lorraine,
and readily in Jerusalem joy shall be realised
for by craft of arms he will recover the cross
and be crowned the King with holy chrism.

The nightmare is interpreted

In his day no other duke shall be dealt such destiny
nor suffer such sorrow as the story unfolds.

'So fortune calls you forward to fulfil your role
and be named in the nine of the noblest on earth.
Royal knights shall read this in the writings of romance:
you shall be rated and reckoned by lords of rank,
and on Doomsday be worshipped for your deeds of warfare
as the worthiest warrior to dwell in the world.
So clerks and kings will declare your exploits
and in the chronicles your triumphs will be treasured for
    eternity.
But the wolves in the woods and the wild beasts
are the rabble of rebels who rise up in your realm,
marauding and making mayhem in your absence
with foreign hosts from far-flung fields.
Within ten days' time you will have tidings, I tell you,
that strife has struck since you strayed from home.
I encourage you to confess all your callous crimes
or those heinous acts will return to haunt you.
Reform, before misfortune finds you, sir,
and pray you find pity for the peace of your soul.'

Then the King arose and reached for his robes,
a jacket of red roses, that most royal flower,
then neck armour and body armour and a beautiful belt,
and he hauled a hood of vivid scarlet on his head
and a hat from the Orient of the highest order,
studded with pearls and precious stones.
His gloves gleamed golden and the edges glinted

The sage predicts misfortune

with grains of rubies, glorious and rare.
Then with hound and sword and no other at his side
he went fast across the fields with fury in his heart,
followed a footpath by the fringe of the forest,
then alone, by a thoroughfare, stood lost in thought.

And as the sun rose in the sky, he saw approaching,
heading towards Rome by the rapidest road,
a fellow in full cloak and flowing clothes,
and a hat, and high and handsome boots.
Flattened farthings were affixed to him all over;
his hems were hung with tassels and trimmings,
and with his purse and skirted mantle, and scallop shells by
    the score,
and his staff and his palm, he appeared to be a pilgrim.
The man's greeting was a grand 'Good morning',
and our Sovereign responded in rough Roman speech,
gave a lordly reply in the language of Latin.
'Wayfarer, why are you wandering here alone
with the whole world at war? Be warned, there is danger.
An enemy army is hidden within that vineyard,
and I swear, if they spot you, sorrow will be yours.
Unless you come with safe conduct from the King himself
knaves will knife you and leave you with nothing,
and if you hold to this highway they won't hesitate to ambush
    you,
unless his honoured knights are on hand to help.'

    Then Sir Craddock spoke to the King himself:
'I shall forgive him my death, so help me God,

          Arthur meets a pilgrim on the road

any warrior who walks in this world under Him.
If the King's fiercest fighter should fly at me in combat
I would encounter him courteously, so Christ have my soul.
And you yourself shall not stall or stop me,
for all you are arrayed in such rich robes.
No war could deter me from wandering where I wish
and no knight either who makes his home on this earth.
So on this path I will pass on my pilgrimage to Rome
to purchase a pardon from the Pope himself
and be purified to be spared the pains of Purgatory.
Then I shall seek out my Sovereign lord at the soonest,
Sir Arthur of England, that excellent King,
for he is actually in this empire, so I hear from true men,
at arms in the east with his eager knights.'
'Where have you come from,' the King questioned,
'to know of King Arthur and his noble knights?
Did you call on him at court when he lodged in his country?
The way of your words brings warmth to my heart.
Your wanderings are worthwhile, and you seek wisely,
for your tongue tells me you are a true British knight.'

'I should know the King, he is my noble kinsman,
and I was chosen in his court as a knight of his chamber,
Sir Craddock I was called in his royal company,
his trusted captain at the castle of Caerleon.
Now I'm chased from my country with a chill in my heart,
and those battlements are seized by bandits from abroad.'

Then our kind King clasped him in his arms,
cast off his kettle-hat and kissed him courteously.

Arthur welcomes Sir Craddock

'Sir Craddock, by Christ you are welcome,' he cried.
'But kindred cousin, you bring cold to my heart.
How goes it in Britain with my brave brothers?
Are they butchered or burned, or broken from life?
Describe, in good faith, how fate unfolded.
What you tell me I shall trust, for I know you to be true.'
'Sir, your warden has been wild and unwarranted in his deeds,
and has worked great wickedness since you went away.
He has captured castles and wears the crown of the King,
and the revenues of the Round Table he has raided for himself.
He has taken all the territories and partitioned them at will,
dubbing and making dukes of the dreaded Danes
who sacked and destroyed many cities as they spread.
With Saracens and Saxons signed up on every side
he has assembled a great army of enemy hosts:
sovereigns of Surgenale and mercenary soldiers;
Picts, pagans and proven knights
of Ireland and Argyll, and outlaws of the Highlands.
Every upstart from the uplands is operating as a knight
and is leader and lord to act as he likes.
And Sir Childrick is chosen as one of his chieftains,
who exploits and oppresses your people with his pack:
they rob your monks and ravage your nuns
and pounce on the poor, pillaging and plundering.
From the Humber to Hawick the upper hand is his.
All the countryside of Kent is assigned to his keep,
every kingly castle which belonged to the crown,
and its copses and wild woods and the walls of its white cliffs,
all that Hengest and Horsa held in their era.
In the Solent off Southampton stand seven score ships

Arthur learns of Mordred's treachery

filled with fierce folk from foreign lands
who will attack your troops the moment you return.
But one more word, for worse news follows:
he has wedded Guinevere and declares her his wife,
and his domain is the margins of the western marches,
and he has got her with child, so the gossip goes;
more than anyone on earth may woe be to him,
that regent not worthy to watch over women.
Thus Sir Mordred has marred and demeaned us all,
so I trekked across the mountains to tell you this truth.'

Then the honoured King, with ire in his heart
at this fall in fortune, lost all colour in his face.
'By the Rood,' said the royal, 'I shall reap my revenge.
He shall repent and pay for his faithless plotting.'
And weeping with woe he went to his tents.
Then the wise monarch woke his sleeping warriors,
roused them with a clarion, kings and every rank,
called them to council and recounted the tale:
'Despite my true deeds I am betrayed with treason,
all my actions were for nothing and my efforts led nowhere.
This treacherous villain will be trounced by trouble
once I track him to his lair, as I am a true lord.
And truly this is Mordred, the man I most trusted!
He has captured my castles and crowned himself King,
and revels in the revenues of the Round Table.
He has formed a retinue from wretches and renegades
and divided my lands amongst dubious lords,
among Saracens and foreign soldiers of fortune.
And he has wedded Guinevere and boasts she is his bride,

Arthur vows revenge

and if he fathers a child then our fortune falls further.
On the sea are assembled seven score ships
full of foreign foe to fight with my forces.
So to Britain the Great we must go at great speed,
to punish this impostor who has put us in peril.
Only fighters whose horses are fresh will follow,
and those hardened by action, my most honoured men.
Sir Howell and Sir Hardolf shall remain behind
to be lords of the lands that belong to my name.
In Lombardy be alert to any change of allegiance
and in Tuscany attend to my task with attention.
Raise rent and revenue from Rome as falls due;
take possession of the city on the day that was assigned,
or those hostages we hold shall be hanged high
from its outer walls, all of them at once.'

Then the bold King made busy with his best knights,
and at the blaring of a bugle the party departed.
They tracked through Tuscany never tarrying on the trek,
and only lingered in Lombardy when the light was lost.
They marched over mountains, through marvellous passes,
strode through Germany, steering a straight route,
then moved forward into Flanders, that fearsome force.
Within fifteen days his fleet was fully fitted,
and soon he set sail, delaying not a second,
shearing through sharp winds and shining waves.

With ropes, by the rock-face, he rode at anchor;
his fiendish foe were afloat on the flood
with ships that were shackled with chariot-chains

Arthur and his knights sail for England

and full to the brim with fierce fighters:
heathens hunkered under every hatch.
Riding high at the rear, crests and helmets
were proudly depicted on painted cloths,
all pinned together piece by piece
in firm fabrics so their size seemed fuller.
Thus the dreaded Danes had dressed their vessels
so no darting arrow could hit or hurt them.

Then our Ruler, robed in royal red,
arrayed the Round Table's ranks in their ships.
That day he dubbed knights and dealt out dukedoms,
had his boats and barges dredge up small boulders,
stretched out many slings in the topcastle to his suiting,
and all crossbows were bent back, primed for battle.
Those attending the catapults tautened the tackle,
jagged bronze heads were joined to the projectiles,
gear for the garrisons was gathered up and stockpiled –
piercing steel pikes and sturdy iron staffs.
On stern after stern stood strong men of arms
with their sleek lances lifted aloft.
Lords and other men were lined up leeward
with painted shields in place on the portside,
while high on the hind-decks stood helmeted knights.
So they shifted for position on the shining sea,
and each man in his gear and his garb seemed to glow.

Our brave King was rowed back and forth in his barge,
bareheaded for battle with his beaver-coloured locks;
a servant bore his sword and his beaten-steel helmet

The British encounter the enemy fleet

with its splendid mantle set with silver mail,
encompassed with a coronal, exquisitely crafted.
He sailed by each ship, stirring men's souls,
and to Clegis and Cleremond he cried out loudly,
'Be guided by the greatness of Gawain and Galyran!'
To Lot and Lionel and Lancelot of the Lake
he announced these noble words as he neared them:
'We shall conquer this country whose coasts are our own,
and the blood of those dogs shall drain in dread;
butcher them on the boats then burn their bodies,
hew out their hearts, those heathen hounds,
they are the issue of harlots, now be led by my hand!'

Then he boarded his own warship and weighed anchor,
donned his shining helmet with the shimmering mail,
and unrolled and raised up his royal-red banners
gloriously crafted with crisp golden crowns.
But in pride of place on his shield shone a Maiden
with an infant in Her arms, the most honoured in all heaven,
for through chase and challenge his faith was unchanged;
such was Arthur's honesty while he lived on this earth.
Then the mariners and the masters of the ships shouted out,
and mate called to mate with mirth in their voices,
stating how things stood and what lay in store.
They tugged on the trusses and tightened the sheets,
hoisted up bonnet-sails and battened the hatches,
brandished bright swords and filled their trumpets with
    breath,
stood proudly at the prow and steered from the stern,
striking across waves to where the strife would start.

Arthur prepares his men for the attack

When a wild, gusty wind rose out of the west
each blast and bluster made the sails bulge,
and the storm caused ship to slam against ship
so that bilge and beam were broken apart,
and prows and sterns were pounded and struck
till the planks to the starboard side were in pieces,
and cog after cog, and cutters and skiffs,
cast grapples across, as the occasion required.
Then head-ropes were hewn which held up the masts,
and vessels were crippled as they crashed and cracked.
Great ships of war shuddered and shattered,
many cabins were smashed and cables cleaved.

     Then knights and fierce fighters killed their foe,
and topcastles were torn down with terrifying weapons,
those prominent towers which were so proudly painted.
With a sideways slash they scythed at the stays
so each swing of the sword made the mainmast sway
and the first one to topple fell on many fellows
so men at the fore went to meet their maker.
They battled bitterly with brutal weaponry;
then assailing sailors swarmed onto warships
from nearby boats, and were bombarded with stones,
but beat back brave men and broke through the hatches.
Some ardent heroes, for all their fine armour
were slotted on iron spikes and made the weapons slimy.
The English archers let fly eagerly,
and their arrows struck harm through the hardest steel,
and so wholly hurt were the heathen knights,
with their armour holed, that they would never be healed.

The battle at sea

Then our forces came forward in the fight with spears,
with those famed for their fierceness surging to the front,
every man there making the most of his might
in that war on the water, with their fatal weapons.
Thus they dealt that day, those newly dubbed knights,
till all the Danes were dead and thrown in the deep.
Then the Britons broke out and went battling ahead,
swooping on noble sailors with their swords,
and when those warriors from other lands leapt to the water
all our lords began laughing out loud at once.

By now spears were splintered and ships were shattered;
Spaniards had sprung smartly over the side;
many keen and courageous knights and their comrades
were killed cold-dead and cast into the deep,
squires lay squashed, their life-blood squandered,
heathens jumped in horror as the ocean heaved
and sank in the salt-sea, seven hundred at a stroke.
So good Sir Gawain had grabbed the prize,
and all those grand galleys he granted to his generals –
Sir Garyn, Sir Griswold and other great lords.
With honourable Galuth he beheaded his enemies.
So the foe's fleet floundered on the floodtide,
and all those false foreigners were flung to their fate.

Yet the traitor was on land, with tried and trusted knights,
trotting about in their trimmings to the blowing of trumpets,
on the shimmering shore with their shining shields,
and Mordred did not shrink but showed himself without
    shame.

Mordred is spotted on the coast

Then King Arthur and Gawain looked onwards together
and saw sixty thousand soldiers marching into sight.
Many fellows had been felled and the floodtide had ebbed,
and now the channels were so silted and swampy with sludge
that in such low-lying water the King was loathe to land,
so stayed at sea to save his steeds from the quicksand,
and look after his liegemen and loyal knights
so the lives of the lamed might be saved and not lost.

     Then good Sir Gawain took charge of a galley
and glided up a gulley with a group of armed men;
where he went aground he waded through the water,
walked girdle-deep in his gleaming gold garb,
and strode onto the sand in sight of those lords,
just himself and his entourage, though it hurts me to say so.
With his bold heraldic banners and his best arms
he bounded up the banking in his bright colours,
and to his banner-bearer he said, 'Go briskly
at that broad battalion massed on the embankment,
and by my faith I shall follow at your feet;
see you swoon from no sword nor shrink from any weapon,
but drag down the doughtiest and deliver them from daylight.
Don't be intimidated by their taunts but stand tall.
You have borne my banners in many a great battle,
we shall fell those false men, and let the Fiend have their souls.
Fight fiercely with this foe and the field shall be ours.
Should I overturn him, woe betide the traitor
who contrived a treason against my true lord.
Out of such circumstances any joy will be scant
as the fight to follow will confirm without doubt.'

Gawain launches a mission

Then that band of stalwarts streamed across the strand,
tearing at those troops and attacking with intent,
piercing men's skin through their shining shields
and splintering lances with spikes and spears.
Fatal wounds they fetched with their fearful weapons,
till many lay dead in the damp of the dew:
dukes and nobles and newly-dubbed knights,
Denmark's most daunting, were forever undone.
In rage, our ranks went on ripping and riving,
slashing at the strongest with unstoppable strokes
and thrusting to the earth in the thick of the throng
the most thorough warriors, three-hundred at a throw!
And Gawain, in his ire, could not harness his anger,
but swiped up a spear and went speeding at a soldier
bearing splendid scarlet spotted with silver;
with his lance he thrust right through him at the throat,
so the honed spear-point splintered on impact
and from that lusty blow the man lost his life.
It was the King of Gotland, a great man of combat.
The remaining foe seemed to flee from the field,
vanquished by the verve of valiant knights,
who moved now on the middle-ranks commanded by Mordred,
our men marching to meet them, and more was the pity,
for had Gawain made ground and gained the green hill
his success had been certain and assured for ever.

But Gawain in his wisdom watched and waited
to root out the wrongdoer whose unruliness led to war,
and through the mass of his men he made for Sir Mordred,
with the Montagues at his side and other mighty soldiers.

Gawain leads the attack

Sir Gawain was furious, and by the force of his will
he levelled a long lance and bellowed loudly:
'False bastard beast, let the Fiend have your bones.
Foulness upon you, felon, and your fake ways.
For your undignified deeds you shall drop to your death,
or I shall die this day, if my destiny is to do so.'

    Then his enemy and his host, that hired army,
ensnared our excellent knights in a circle,
who were tricked and trapped by that treacherous traitor.
Dukes of Denmark were quick to do their duty,
and leaders from Lithuania with their many legions,
surrounding our soldiers with their spears at the ready;
outlaws and Saracens from over the ocean,
sixty thousand warmongers lying in wait,
came swooping swiftly on our seven score knights
in sudden deceit by the salt-laden sea.
Then Gawain's grey eyes were wet with weeping
out of grief for the good men he had guided thus far,
for he saw they were wounded and wearied by war,
and his wits failed him, so woeful he felt.
Then he sighed, and with tears streaming he said:
'We are besieged by Saracens on every side.
I sigh not for my own skin, so help me our Saviour,
but am sorrowful to see how we are suddenly besieged.
Be dutiful this day and those dukes shall be yours,
and never doubt our Deity or dread any weapon.
We shall exit this escapade as most excellent knights,
and find endless ecstasy with heaven's bright angels.
Though unwittingly we have wasted ourselves in this way,

Gawain's party is surrounded

our work shall do us well in the worship of Christ.
I swear on my word, these Saracens shall ensure
that we will solemnly sup with our Saviour in paradise,
in the presence of the precious and peerless Prince,
with prophets and patriarchs and noble apostles,
before his fair-featured face, who fathered all mankind.
He who yields to those mares' sons who mass over yonder
while there is life in his hands or heat in his heart
shall never be saved or be succoured by Christ
but sink into hell, and Satan have his soul.'

Grimly Sir Gawain gripped his weapon,
steeled himself and went striding into the struggle.
Swiftly he set straight the chains of his sharp sword
and shoved out his shield, not shirking from the task,
throwing caution to the wind as he waded into combat,
wounding many warriors with withering blows
so blood spurted and splashed as he slashed his way through.
And though his woes weighed heavy he hardly wavered,
but in the worship of his lord he unleashed great wrath.
In the mayhem he stabbed steeds and struck at stalwarts,
so stern men were left strapped in their stirrups stone-dead.
He rived open rude steel and ran through chain-mail,
and no fighter could deflect him, for his senses had flown.
With a furious heart he fell into a frenzy,
felling any foe who stood before him;
no fated man ever found such fortune in fight.
He went hammering headlong at the whole host,
harming and hurting the hardiest in the world;
lion-like he launched his lethal attacks,

Gawain fights ferociously

leaving lords and leaders lifeless on the land.
And Sir Gawain never paused, despite his despair,
but went on wounding warriors with wondrous strokes,
as if well aware that he would waste himself.
So wayward was his will that his wits failed,
and like a crazed creature he clattered into those closest,
and where he went, in that way, all wallowed in blood,
so every foe knew his fate from the felling of his fellows.
Then he moved against Sir Mordred in the middle of his
    knights,
hammered him heartily and holed his shield,
but the sly one shimmied around the sharp sword
and sliced open his short-ribs by the width of a span.
The shaft shivered as it shot through that shining knight,
and the blood that he shed streamed straight to his shanks,
and boldly shone on his burnished shin-plates.
So they battled and brawled, and Mordred was bowled over
with the lunge of a lance, landing on his shoulders,
and lay heaped across the earth, horribly injured.
Then Gawain followed fiercely, fell on him in fury,
but his rage was too great for grace to treat him gladly,
for he drew a short knife sheathed in silver
to slice the man's throat, but couldn't thrust right through,
and his hand slipped aslant, went skimming off the chain-mail,
and the other underhandedly hit him from below;
with a stropped blade that traitor struck his blow
through helmet and head, high into the brain;
and thus Gawain was gone, that good man of arms,
without a hand to help him, and huge is the pity.
Gone, Sir Gawain, who guided many men,

Mordred kills Gawain

from Gower to Guernsey, all the great lords
of Glamorgan and Wales, all the great warriors:
having glimpsed such grief, no joy will they regain.

Then King Frederick of Friesland, in good faith,
asked that false fellow about our fierce fighter:
'Did you know the name of that knight of your land?
Say if you can what kin he came from,
and what warrior he was with his wondrous armour
and his griffin of gold, who now lies on the ground.
He grieved us greatly, so help me God,
bringing down our best men and doing us great damage.
He was the sternest and staunchest who ever wore steel,
for he trounced our troops, destroying them forever.'

Then Sir Mordred was moved to mouth this tribute:
'He was unmatched in this world, I admit it; that man
was good Sir Gawain, the greatest of mortals
and most gracious of lords who lived under God.
A man fierce of fist, favoured in warfare,
honoured in hall above all under heaven,
the lordliest of leaders for as long as he lived,
loudly lionised in lands near and far.
Had you known him, Sir King, in his native country,
his craft and his courtesy and his kindly works,
his bravery and boldness and his deeds in battle,
his death you would lament all the days of your life.'

Tears flowed from that traitor's face,
and his tongue was silent, till suddenly he turned

Mordred pays tribute to Gawain

and went away weeping, woeful at that time
that destiny should deal him such a devastating hand.
Just to ponder his predicament pierced his heart,
and he sighed with sorrow for his kin's sake as he rode.
And when that mutinous man had mind to remember
the reputation and the triumphs of the Round Table,
he felt guilt and disgust for his regrettable deeds.
He waited no longer, went at once with his weapons
out of fear of our great King, in case he should come.

He hurried to Cornwall, haunted in his heart
by the cousin he had killed, who lay cold on the coast.
He trembled with terror, waiting for tidings,
then the following Tuesday the traitor made tracks,
with a trick up his sleeve, intent on treason.
By the tidal Tamar he pitched his tent,
and immediately commanded that a messenger take a missive,
sending word to Guinevere that the world had changed
since the King had made the crossing to his fair country
and fought with his forces, felling them in the flood.
He advised her to fly, to flee far with her children,
till he could slip away unseen then seek her out and speak to her;
to hurry to Ireland's empty outer mountains,
and to live in the lonely wilderness of those wastelands.

In York where she waited she wept and wailed;
she groaned with grief, and her tears were great.
Passing from the palace, her principal maidens
accompanied her in her carriage, chasing towards Chester;
she was dressed as if for death, with dread in her heart.

Mordred flees to Cornwall

And advanced then to Caerleon, and with vows took the veil,
requested the habit in honour of Christ,
but out of falsehood and fraud, and in fear of her husband.

When our wise King learned that Gawain had landed,
he writhed about with hurt and wrung his hands,
and ordered launches to be lowered in the low water,
and came ashore, lion-like, with his leading lords,
slipping in the mudflats, slime up to his middle,
yet he strode on strongly with his sword drawn,
urging on his army, banners held high,
and with anger in his heart went hurtling across wide sands,
pressing forward to the field where the dead lay fallen.
Of the traitor's men on their mounts with their trappings,
ten thousand were slain if the truth be told,
and on our side, for certain, only seven score knights
had lost their lives, along with their leader.
The King courteously turned over both comrades and enemy,
Earls of Africa and Austrian soldiers,
men of Orkney and Argyll, kings of Ireland,
Norway's noblest in huge numbers,
Danish dukes and newly dubbed knights,
and the King of Gotland in gaudy garb,
who lay groaning on the ground, gored through his guts.
Our King kept on hunting with a heavy heart,
tracking down the true ranks of the Round Table;
they were heaped on the earth, piled on their own
with slaughtered Saracens encircling the scene,
and good Sir Gawain in his glinting gear,
face down in the field, fists full of grass,

Arthur searches for Gawain's body

his bold red banners brought to the floor,
his sword and broad shield swimming with blood.
Never was our Sovereign so saddened and sorrowful,
or so sunk in his spirits as he was at that sight.

The Sovereign stared, stricken with horror;
he groaned with grief and wept great tears.
Then he knelt to the corpse and clasped his comrade,
cast up his visor and quickly kissed him,
looked at his eyelids which were locked shut
and at his lead-like lips and lifeless white face,
then the crowned King let out a loud cry:
'Dearest kin of my kind, I am cut to the core,
for now my honour is hollow and my war over.
All my hope, my health, my fortune in arms,
and my heart and hardiness rested wholly on him.
My counsel, my comfort, the keeper of my cares.
He was captain among knights who lived under Christ,
and worthy to be King, though I wore the crown.
My wealth and worth throughout this wide world
were won by Sir Gawain through his wisdom alone.
For pity,' said Arthur, 'such pain overpowers me;
I am utterly laid low in my own land.
Oh dire, dreadful death, you drag your heels.
Why dawdle and draw back? You drown my heart.'

Then the sweet King swayed and fell in a swoon,
then staggered and stood and stooped to kiss him,
till his noble beard was bright with blood,
as if he had bent to butcher a beast.

Arthur mourns the loss of Gawain

Had Sir Ewain and leading lords arrived any later
the blow would have burst his bold heart right there.

'Cease,' the lords said, 'for you do yourself no service.
Such heartache is unending and can never be healed.
There is no honour to be had in the wringing of hands,
and to weep as a woman is deemed unworthy.
Be kingly of countenance, as the crown demands,
and put a close to this clamour, for the love of heavenly
    Christ.'

'By His blood,' said the Sovereign, 'I shall not stop
till my brain lies broken or my breast burst.
Such a skewering sadness never sank to my heart.
And my misery is more because that man was kin.
No more sorrowful sight have I seen with my eyes.
Pure and clean, he lies cold, on account of my sin.'

Down knelt the King, and called out his keening;
throwing care to the wind he cried these words:
'Oh heavenly God, behold this grief;
the earth runs red with his royal blood.
Shrouded, it should be, and enshrined in gold,
for it lacks all sin, so save me our Lord.'

The Sovereign stooped, distraught at heart,
cupped the blood kindly in his clean hands,
cast it in a kettle-hat and covered it carefully,
then bore the corpse to his kinsman's birthplace.

Arthur's sorrow

'Here I make my oath,' was the King's utterance,
'to the Messiah and to Mary, that mild Queen of heaven:
I shall never again hunt, or set harrying hounds
upon roe deer or reindeer that run upon the earth,
or let greyhound glide or goshawk fly,
or see fowl felled that flap on the wing;
and no falcon or formel shall I handle on my fist,
or join, on this earth, in the joys of the gyrfalcon,
or reign as royalty, or host my Round Table,
till my dear man's death is duly avenged.
But listless will lie still while my life lasts,
till our Deity and death have done what they will.'

Then with care in their hearts they caught up the corpse
and carried it on a courser, accompanied by the King,
and went to Winchester by the swiftest way,
weary, woeful, and with wounded knights.
The prior of that monastery and his monks of pure morals
passed in procession as they greeted the Prince,
who bestowed on their brotherhood the bold knight's body.

'See him cared for courteously and kept in the kirk,
have dirges sung, such as the dead are due,
and sweeten them with masses for the sake of his soul.
See no candles are absent, nor any other honour,
and that the body be embalmed and laid on a bier.
If you keep to that covenant, you may claim reward
when I come here again, if Christ so decrees it.
But bury him not till they are beaten and brought down
who dealt us woe and dragged us into war.'

Arthur swears to take revenge

Then Sir Wicher, a wise warrior, spoke these words:
'Act warily if your wishes are to work out well:
stay on in this city and assemble your soldiers,
secure in their company and safe in these streets.
Bring knights from their countries who are keepers of castles,
and bring good men of arms from the greatest garrisons.
For in faith, we are too few in force to fight them,
those scores of men we saw massing on the mainland.'

Then the Sovereign spoke these stern words:
'Have no doubts, I pray you, nor dread any danger:
single-handed, just myself, one soul beneath the sun,
should I set sight upon him and seize him in my hands,
in the middle of his men I should maul him to death
before stepping half a steed's-length away from that spot.
Among his fellows I shall fall on him and finish him forever.
And so I swear my solemn vow devoutly to my Saviour
and to his mother Mary, the mild Queen of heaven.
I shall not stop or be stalled or find stillness in my heart
in any city or suburb which is set upon this earth,
and never slumber or sleep, though my eyes weigh like stones,
till the slayer be slain, and through my strength lies slaughtered,
and have pursued those pagans who so pained my people
and imprisoned and punished them in what place I please.'

Among the ranks of the Round Table none could rein or
    arrest him,
or pacify that prince with pleasant words,
and no faithful follower could meet his face,
so lordly he looked at the loss of his knights.

Arthur refuses to be pacified

Then he dallied no longer but left for Dorset,
stricken by sorrow, I swear, with tears streaming,
and entered into Cornwall with anguish in his heart,
tracking and trailing every trace of that villain,
turning by the Tamar as he sought the traitor,
and the following Friday he found him in a forest;
stepping from the stirrups of his steed he cried out,
and took to the field with his fellow fighters.

Then the enemy issued from under the canopy,
with an alien host, heinous to the eye;
Mordred the Malbranche with the mass of his army,
his forces moving forward in formation from the forest
in seven great squadrons suitably equipped,
sixty thousand soldiers, a startling spectacle,
all fighting folk from foreign fields,
their frontline finely formed near those fresh streams.
And the whole of Arthur's army, his host of knights,
was just eighteen hundred who were entered in the rolls,
massively under-manned, but for Christ's might,
to march against that multitude and meet them in the
    meadows.

Then the royal ruler of the Round Table
rode upon his steed and readied his ranks,
arrayed his vanguard to advantage, as of right;
Sir Ewain and Sir Erik and other great earls
took masterly command of the middle ranks thereafter
alongside Merrak and Meneduke, mighty in muscle;
Idrus and Alymer, their youthful allies,

stood beside Arthur with seven score men.
Then rapidly he arranged the men of the rearguard,
the most lively lot of the lords of the Order,
and when the ranks were right he roared his battle-cry,
inspiring his soldiers with a Sovereign's speech:

'I beseech you, sirs, for the sake of our Saviour,
that you do well today, and dread no weapon.
Fight fiercely now and defend yourselves,
fell those ill-fated folk, and the field shall be ours.
They are Saracens on that side, sweep them asunder.
Set on them without sympathy, for the sake of our Lord,
and if today on this earth we are destined to die
we shall be hoisted into heaven before we are half cold.
Let no warrior stand in the way of lordly work,
but lay those lads low till their game is lost.
Pay no attention to my life nor believe any lie,
but be busy near my banners with your bright weapons;
let my sternest knights be a stronghold to those streamers
and hold them up high so they are visible to all;
if wrenched down by some wretch, then rescue and raise them.
Now put my words to work, for my war ends today.
My pleasure or my pain – it is yours to please.
May Christ, honour-crowned, bring comfort to you all,
as the kindliest creatures that a king ever led.
With all the worth of my will I wish on you my blessings
and to all bold Britons, may the bliss be yours.'

At the prime of morning they piped their approach,
peerless stalwarts, set to prove their strength.

149   *Arthur's rousing speech to his men*

Boldly the buglers filled their trumpets with breath,
and cornets sounded sweetly where knights assembled.
Then the gentle knights joined in battle with joy,
and judged it the most just of their journeys to war,
as brave Britons embraced their shields
and crossed themselves with Christ, their spears set to clash.

   Then Sir Arthur's host spied the enemy army,
and went lunging with their shields, delaying no longer,
thrusting forward at the foe with full-throated cries,
shattering shining shields wherever they struck.
Rapidly the true regiments of the Round Table
slashed through strong mail with sleek steel,
burst through armour and broke bright helmets,
hewed down heathens and hacked them at the neck.
Blood flowed freely among the flashing silver.
Lying felled, the foe's fiercest were fierce no longer.
But heathens of Argyll and Irish kings
enveloped our vanguard with venomous men:
Picts and pagans with perilous weapons,
piercing our knights with their pitiless pikes,
mowing down the mightiest with mortal blows.
They caused harm to our host by holding their ways;
so ferociously they rioted and rucked to all sides
that much blood spilt from the bodies of brave Britons,
and none dared ride to the rescue for all the riches of this
   realm,
for the foe was reinforced by fighters on all fronts.
Our King stirred not one step, but stood his ground,
and destroyed three lines with his strength alone.

The two armies clash

'Idrus,' cried Arthur, 'go elsewhere with your help.
I see Sir Ewain set upon by savage Saracens.
Ready yourself to arrange his rescue.
Go swiftly with stern men to assist your father,
set in on them from the side and bring succour to those lords,
for my sadness shall not subside till they are safe and sound.'

Idrus gave Arthur his earnest answer:
'In faith, he is my father, and I should never fail him.
He has fostered and fed me, and my fellow brothers.
But this mission I must miss, so help me my Maker,
and cast aside all kinship for you alone, my King.
I never broke or breached his bidding for any man,
but was blissfully obedient like a beast to his keeper,
and he commanded me with kind and courteous words
to be loyal to you alone, and to no other lord.
So his command I shall keep, if Christ will allow it.
He is older than I, but we both shall meet our end.
He shall fall first, and I will soon follow.
If he is destined to die this day upon earth,
may our rightly crowned Christ take care of his soul.'

Then the royal King railed, with a rueful heart,
lifted his hands high and looked to the heavens:
'Why has our Deity, through deed of his dear will,
not deemed that today I should die for you all?
I would choose that loss, than for all my life be lord
of all that Alexander once owned on this earth.'

Sir Ewain and Sir Erik, those excellent knights,

Sir Idrus remains at Arthur's side

held firm against the enemy, hitting out eagerly;
the heathens of Orkney and the Irish kings
they gashed and gored with their great swords,
hacking at those hulks with their hard weapons,
laying lords low with lusty strikes.
Shoulders bearing shields they shredded to their haunches,
and through many men's mail they maimed and mauled.
No earthly king was so honoured in arms
on his last day alive as Arthur alone.
But the day was a drought that dried their hearts,
and drinkless they both died, and dreadful was the doing.

Now our middle-guard marched in, mixing and merging
with the many men of Sir Mordred the Malbranche;
he had hidden at the rear, at the edge of the holt,
with his army on the heath, and harm it would bring us,
for he had watched the warfare, the way it all went,
what our chivalry had achieved through armed challenge,
and how our forces were flagging and were soon to fall,
and quickly he decided to encounter our King.
And that devious double-crosser had ditched his own banner –
the engrailed saltire – and had snatched up instead
three silver lions which he lifted aloft,
passant on purple, with proud and prized jewels.
And so the King would not recognise the cunning wretch
the coward bore no cloth, so carried no device.
But our monarch immediately had the measure of the man,
and calmly to Sir Cador he declared these words:
'I see the felon comes forward at a fair pace;
that lad with the lions looks a lot like him!

Arthur sees through Mordred's disguise

If he rides within reach he shall meet with ruin,
for all his treason and trickery, as I am the true lord.
Today Clarent and Excalibur shall be called upon to prove
which is keener where it carves and cleaner where it cuts.
Mettle shall be tested where metal meets mail.
It was my treasured protector, true and trusted,
kept for the crowning of anointed kings;
on days when I dubbed either dukes or earls
it was borne boldly by its bright hilt;
I never dared harm it in deeds of arms
but cared that it stayed clean for my own cause:
but see, Clarent is uncovered, that crown amongst swords,
so my wardrobe at Wallingford has been looted for its worth.
And no one but Guinevere knew where it was;
my wife alone knew the whereabouts of that weapon
and the closed-up coffers which belong to the crown,
with the rings and relics and regalia of France
which were found on Sir Frollo when he fell to his fate.'

Being moved into action, Sir Merrak met Mordred,
hit him mightily with a hammered mace;
the border of his helmet he broke clean off
so bright red blood came running down his breastplate.
Mordred wheeled in pain and his face went white,
but like an embattled boar he returned the blow.
Then he flashed the sword of shining silver
that was Arthur's own, and was Uther's, his father,
which was held in high honour in the arsenal at Wallingford;
and the dismal dog dealt out such dreaded dints
that withdrawing was all that the other dare do.

Sir Merrak engages Mordred

For Sir Merrak was a man who was marred by age
and Sir Mordred was mighty and at the peak of manliness.
No one, even a knight, could come within the compass
of the sweep of that sword, or their lifeblood would spill.

Our King watched this happen, and hastened into action,
went forward through the fray by force of his strength,
met with Sir Mordred, and spoke with maddened heart:
'Turn, untrue traitor, your time has come.
By great God, your existence by my hands shall be ended.
All the riches of the realms shall not rescue you from death.'

The King brought Excalibur crashing down,
shearing off cleanly the corner-piece of his shield
and slashing a six-inch wound to his shoulder,
spattering his chain-mail with shimmering scarlet blood.
He shuddered and shook, shrank back just a little,
but then shockingly and sharply in his shining armour
the felon struck forcefully with his fine sword,
slicing through the rib-plates to our Sovereign's side;
through hauberk and heavy armour he opened him up
with a wound to his flesh half a foot wide.
He had dealt him his deathblow, and how dreadful it was
that this dear man should die but for our Deity's will.

Yet with Excalibur he executed an exacting stroke,
thrust his fine shield forward in an act of offence
then slashed off his enemy's sword-hand as he swooped;
an inch from the elbow he hacked it clean off,
chopping through the shining armguard and chain-mail,

Arthur fatally wounded by Mordred

so he swooned on the spot then swayed and sank,
and his hand and hilt lay still upon the earth.

Then eagerly Arthur opened his enemy's visor
and buried the bright blade in his body to the handle,
and he squirmed as he died, skewered on the sword.
'It sorrows me, I swear,' said our doomed Sovereign,
'that such a false offender should have so fair a death.'

When their fight was finished, then the field was won,
and all the forces of the foe were left to their fate.
They fled to the forest and fell among the groves
as our fierce fighters followed on their heels,
hunted and hacked down those heathen dogs,
murdered Sir Mordred's mercenaries in the mountains;
no child or chieftain escaped their chase,
and to track them and trample them caused little trouble.

But in the aftermath, when Sir Arthur found Sir Ewain's
    body,
and Sir Erik the esteemed and other great lords,
he gathered up Sir Cador, engulfed with grief,
and Sir Clegis and Sir Cleremond, those comrades in arms,
and Sir Lot and Sir Lionel, Sir Lancelot and Lowes,
and Merrak and Meneduke, the mightiest ever,
then mournfully he laid out his lords upon the land,
looked upon their corpses, and called out inconsolably,
like a man lost to life, to whom all love lies hidden.
He felt faint and stumbled as all his strength failed,
and his eyes turned heavenwards and his face altered;

Arthur sends Mordred to his grave

suddenly he swayed and fell in a swoon,
then climbed to his knees, crying and keening:
'Oh King, truly crowned, with such cares am I left.
All my lords are laid low, strewn on the land,
those who won me gifts by God's own grace,
upheld my high honour through their excellence in arms,
made me a mighty monarch and master of all earth.
In a time of trouble, terror came their way,
and through taint of that traitor, all my trusty men are dead.
Here rests the royal blood of the Round Table,
thrown away on that thief, and through it all comes ruin.
Helpless on this heath I will house myself alone,
like a woeful widow, wanting her man,
and I will wail and weep and wring my hands,
for all my grandeur and glory are gone for good.
I take leave of all lordship for as long as I live.
Here the blood of the Britons is burst from its heart,
and here, in this exploit, all my happiness ends.'

Then the ranks of the Round Table rallied their
    numbers,
riding to the side of their royal ruler,
and quite soon seven score knights were assembled
and surrounded their Sovereign, who was sorely wounded.
Then the crowned King knelt and cried to the company:
'I thank you, God, for your grace in giving us
the virtue and wisdom to vanquish those villains,
and for allowing that such lords would lose in battle.
Not once on this earth did you send us dishonour,
but saw that we held the upper hand against all others.

Arthur's final sorrowing

We cannot loiter here at leisure or look for other lords,
for that craven coward has cut me to the core;
let us go to Glastonbury – we can gain no other good –
where we may rest from harm and let our injuries heal.
And of the dealings of this day, let our Deity be honoured,
who has deemed it our destiny to die in our own land.'

Holding to his orders, all of them at once,
they rode to Glastonbury by the most rapid route;
entering the Isle of Avalon, Arthur alighted
and made for a manor house, for he could travel no more.
A surgeon of Salerno inspected his wounds,
but the Sovereign knew well that he would never be saved,
and soon to his circle he said these words:
'Call for me a confessor with Christ in his hands,
I must receive the sacrament at the soonest moment.
Constantine my cousin, he shall bear the crown,
on account of his kinship, if Christ will allow it.
Break not my blessing that those lords shall be buried
who battled with their blades and were butchered today,
and be merciless and mark that Mordred's children
be slain for good sense then slung in the sea,
so no wicked weed in this world can take root;
I warn you, for your worth, to work as I bid.
I excuse all crimes, for Christ's love of heaven,
and if Guinevere has fared well, let her fate be to flourish.'

He said, 'Into thy hands,' his last utterance upon earth,
then his spirit was spent, and he spoke no more.

Arthur passes away

Then the baronage of Britain, bishops and everyone,
gathered at Glastonbury with grief-stricken hearts,
to bury their bold King, give him back to the earth
with all the majesty and honour that a man might have.
Roundly they rang bells, sang the Requiem,
and said masses and matins with mournful voices.
Religious men, dressed in their richest robes,
pontiffs and prelates in their precious clothes,
dukes and statesmen suited most solemnly,
countesses kneeling and clasping their hands,
frowning ladies lamenting their loss,
brides and daughters draped in black,
they encircled the sepulchre with streaming tears,
for such a sorrowful sight was never seen in their time.

And so ended King Arthur, so the annals state,
who was of Hector's kin, the King of Troy's son,
and of Sir Priam the Prince, praised the world over;
from there the Britons brought his bold forebears
into Britain the Greater, as the book of Brut tells.

Here lies Arthur, the once and future King.

Characters and Names
of the *Alliterative Morte Arthure*

~

Absalom – the biblical character, King David's son
Sir Achinour – a British knight
The Earl of Africa – a Roman ally
Alexander – Alexander the Great, one of the Nine Worthies
Algere – the brother of the Earl of Antele, loyal to Lorraine
Alymer – a British knight
King Angus – the Scottish King, loyal to Arthur
The Earl of Antele – an ally of Lorraine
King Arthur – the King of Britain
Sir Aladuke (of Towell) – a British knight
Askanere – a British knight

Sir Baldwin (also Bishop Baldwin?) – a British knight
Sir Bedivere – a British knight, Arthur's sword-bearer
Sir Berade – a British knight
Sir Berill – a British knight
Sir Boice – a British knight
Sir Brian – a British knight
The Baron of Brittany – an ally of Arthur
The Duchess of Brittany – abducted and murdered by the monster
    of Mont St Michel

The Captain of Corneto – a Roman leader

159

Sir Cador of Cornwall – a British knight, Arthur's sister's son
The Chief Chancellor – a Roman
Charlemagne – historically, the King of the Franks and Emperor of the
    Romans, one of the Nine Worthies
Chastelayne – a young British squire
Sir Cheldrick – an ally of Lorraine
Sir Childrick – an ally of Mordred
Clarent – Arthur's ceremonial sword, stolen by Mordred
Sir Claribald – a British knight
Sir Clegis – a British knight
Sir Clement – a British knight
Sir Cleremond – a British knight
Sir Cleremus – a British knight
Sir Clowdmur – a British knight
Constantine – the son of Sir Cador
Sir Craddock – a British knight
The Countess of Crasine – companion of the Duchess of Lorraine

'the Dauphin' – presumably the crown prince of Lorraine
David – slayer of Goliath in the Old Testament, one of the Nine Worthies
Sir Dolphin the Dauntless – an ally of Lorraine
Sir Erik – a British knight
Sir Ermyngall – a British knight
Sir Evander – an earl of the Orient, Roman ally
Sir Ewain Fitz Henry – a British knight
Sir Ewain Fitz Urien – a British knight
Excalibur – Arthur's sword

Fawnell of Friesland – Sir Florent's horse
Sir Feltemour – a Roman knight
Sir Ferrant – a British knight
Ferrar – a British knight
Sir Ferraunt – a British knight
Sir Florent – a British knight
Sir Floridas – a British knight

160

King Frederick of Friesland – an ally of Mordred
Sir Frederick – an ally of Lorraine
Sir Frollo – a Roman knight killed by Arthur on a previous campaign

Galuth – Sir Gawain's sword
Galyran – a British knight
Sir Garyn – a British knight
Sir Gayous – a Roman, uncle to Lucius
Sir Gawain – one of Arthur's most trusted and loyal knights
Sir Gerard – a Justice of Wales, a British knight
Sir Gerin – a British knight
Godfrey – Godfrey of Bouillon, one of the Nine Worthies
Golapas – a Roman warrior
The King of Gotland – an ally of Mordred
Sir Griswold – a British knight
Guinevere – the Queen, wife of Arthur

Sir Hardolf – a British knight
Hardolf ('the heathen') – an ally of Lorraine
Hector of Troy - one of the Nine Worthies
Hengest – an Anglo-Saxon invader of Britain in earlier times
Sir Herygall – a British knight
Sir Heryll – a British knight
Horsa – an Anglo-Saxon invader of Britain in earlier times
King Howell – the father of the Duchess of Brittany, Arthur's cousin
Sir Howell – one of Arthur's knights, possibly the abovementioned as well

Sir Idrus – a British knight, Sir Ewain's son
Ioneke – a British knight

Jehosaphat's Vale – the site of an adventure from a story of the Crusades
Joatell – a character from a story of the Crusades
Sir Jonathal – a Roman knight
Joshua – the biblical character, one of the Nine Worthies
Sir Judas – Judas Maccabeus, one of the Nine Worthies

Julian of Genoa – an ally of Lorraine

Julius - a character from a story of the Crusades

Julius Caesar – the historical Roman leader, one of the Nine Worthies

Sir Kay – a British knight, Arthur's cup-bearer

Sir Lancelot (of the Lake) – a British knight

Sir Leo – a Roman ally

Lewlin – a British knight

Sir Lionel – a Briton, brother of Lowell

The Lord (or Duke) of Lorraine – an opponent of Arthur

The Duchess of Lorraine – the wife of the Duke/Lord of Lorraine

Lowell – a Briton, brother of Lionel

Lowes – a Briton

Sir Lot – a British knight

Lucius Iberius – the Emperor of Rome

The Marquis of Metz – an ally of Lorraine

The Marshal of France – a French lord who requests military assistance
    from Arthur

Sir Marshall de Mowne – a Roman knight

Sir Mawrelle of Maunces – a British knight

Mawrene – a British knight, brother of Sir Mawrelle

Sir Meneduke of Mentoch – a British knight

Sir Merrak – a British knight

The Lord of Milan (also the Overlord of Milan?) – a surrendering Roman

Sir Mordred (the Malbranche) – Arthur's nephew by his sister

The Nine Worthies – the nine historical and mythological figures thought
    to embody the ideals of chivalry and greatness

Sir Origge – a British knight

Sir Priamus – a knight who defects to the British side after fighting Gawain

Sir Raynald – a British knight, son of Sir Rowland
Raynald of Rhodes – an ally of Lorraine
Sir Richard – a British knight, son of Sir Rowland
The Duke of Rouen – a British ally
Sir Rowland – a British knight, father of Sir Richard and Sir Raynald

Sagramour – a Briton
The Sovereign of Saxony – an ally of Loraine
Senator Barouns – a Roman leader
Senator Peter – a Roman leader
The Senator of Sutri – a Roman leader
The Seneshal of Sutri – a Roman
Sir Sextynour of Libya – a Roman ally
Swyan of Sweden – an ally of Lorraine
The King of Syria – a Roman ally
The Sultan of Syria – a Roman ally

Sir Uhtred – a Roman, the Overlord of Turin
Unwin – a legendary character of old
Sir Uriel – a British knight
Uther (Pendragon) – father of Arthur
Sir Utolf – an earl of the Orient, a Roman ally

Sir Valiant – the Welsh King, loyal to Arthur
The Viscount of Rome (also the Viscount of Valence?) – a Roman, an old
    adversary of Valiant

Wade – a legendary warrior of old
Sir Walter – a British knight
Sir Wichard – a British knight
Sir Wicher – a British knight